Look to the East!

A Ritual of the First Degrees of Freemasonry

by

Ralph P. Lester

ISBN: 978-1-63182-009-0

Look to the East!

A Ritual of the First Degrees of Freemasonry

All Rights reserved. No part of this book maybe reproduced without written permission from the publishers, except by a reviewer who may quote brief passages in a review to be printed in a newspaper or magazine.

Printed January, 2014

Published and Distributed By:

Lushena Books
607 Country Club Drive, Unit E
Bensenville, IL 60106
www.lushenabks.com

ISBN: 978-1-63182-996-3

Printed in the United States of America

LOOK TO THE EAST!

A RITUAL
of the
FIRST THREE DEGREES OF MASONRY

Containing
The Complete Work of the Entered Apprentice,
Fellow-craft and Master-mason's Degrees,
with Their Ceremonies, Lectures, etc.

Edited by
RALPH P. LESTER

Revised and Enlarged Edition
with
Forms of Masonic Documents

CONTENTS.

ENTERED APPRENTICE, OR FIRST DEGREE..............
   OPENING THE LODGE...........................
   CALLING A LODGE FROM A HIGHER TO A LOWER DE-
     GREE ....
   OPENING A LODGE OF ENTERED APPRENTICES........
   CEREMONIES OF INITIATION.....................
   ENTERED APPRENTICE LECTURE...................
   CLOSING AN ENTERED APPRENTICES' LODGE.........
   SHORT METHOD FOR THE ABOVE...................
   CALLING OFF AND ON...........................
FELLOW CRAFT, OR SECOND DEGREE....................
   OPENING THE LODGE...........................
   CALLING FROM A HIGHER TO A LOWER DEGREE.......
   OPENING A LODGE OF FELLOW CRAFTS.............
   CEREMONIES OF PASSING........................
   FELLOW CRAFT LECTURE.........................
   CLOSING A LODGE OF FELLOW CRAFTS.............
MASTER MASON, OR THIRD DEGREE....................
   OPENING A LODGE OF MASTER MASONS.............
   ORDER OF BUSINESS............................
   CEREMONIES OF RAISING........................
   MASTER MASON'S LECTURE.......................
   CLOSING A LODGE OF MASTER MASONS.............
   FORMS OF MASONIC DOCUMENTS...................

PREFACE.

It has doubtless been a matter of comment and surprise among the Members of the Fraternity that all the books which are avowedly intended to serve as guides to the Work of a Lodge invariably contain *more or less* than their professed object demands.

They are usually deficient in the very points that may be most needed, rendering the use of a separate Monitor unavoidable; while, on the other hand, they include a great deal of information on matters with which every Mason is necessarily perfectly familiar, and which it is neither needful nor desirable to be communicated to the uninitated.

It has been the aim of the Compiler of this little volume to avoid both these defects: first, by omitting all Passwords, Grips, and other esoteric subjects; and second, by giving the Work of the first three degrees monitorially as well as ritually complete, in plain language for ready reference, and entirely free from the tedious perplexities of cypher or other arbitrary and unintelligible contractions.

LOOK TO THE EAST

ENTERED APPRENTICE, OR FIRST DEGREE.

All matters of business in a Lodge are transacted in the third degree. If a candidate is to be initiated, the Lodge is opened in the third degree; and when, in the regular order of business, the time arrives for the ceremony of initiation to take place, the Lodge is called off in the third degree, and remains so while the first degree is opened.

OPENING A LODGE OF MASTER MASONS.

The ceremony of opening a Lodge in the third degree is conducted as follows: When the regular time for opening has arrived the Master repairs to his station and calls the Lodge to order with one rap of his gavel. The door is shut, the brethren clothe themselves and take their seats; the officers put on their jewels; the Wardens dispose of their columns, down in the West, erect in the South; the Deacons take their rods; the Secretary lays his books and papers and the three Great Lights upon his table, and in a few moments the Lodge is silent and in order for the opening. The Master then proceeds as follows:

ENTERED APPRENTICE, OR FIRST DEGREE.

W. M. to S. W. Brother Senior Warden, proceed to satisfy yourself that all present are Master Masons.

The Senior Warden rises and makes a personal observation of every one that is present. He then requests the Senior and Junior Deacons to give to him, in a whisper, the pass of a Master Mason, and to demand it, under the same conditions, from each person present except the Worshipful Master, Senior Warden and Junior Warden. After this is done, the Junior Deacon communicates the pass to the Senior Deacon and he to the Worshipful Master.

W. M. to S. W. The pass is ———.

S. W. to W. M. All present are Master Masons, Worshipful Master.

When any one addresses the Master during any masonic ceremony, he must rise and salute.

The Worshipful Master calls up the Senior Deacon and Junior Deacon by one rap.

W. M. to J. D. Brother Junior Deacon, what is the first great care of Masons when in Lodge assembled?

J. D. to W. M. To see that the Lodge is duly tyled, Worshipful Master.

W. M. to J. D. Perform that duty. Inform the Tyler that I am about to open a Lodge of Master Masons, and direct him to tyle accordingly.

The Junior Deacon opens the door without knocking, and satisfies himself that the Tyler is at his post, he then communicates to him the Master's orders and shuts the door. The Tyler then locks the door on the outside.

J. D. to W. M. The Lodge is duly tyled, Worshipful Master.

ENTERED APPRENTICE, OR FIRST DEGREE.

W. M. to J. D. How are we tyled, Brother Junior Deacon?

J. D. to W. M. By a brother Master Mason without the door, armed with the proper instrument of his office.

W. M. to J. D. What are his duties there?

J. D. to W. M. To keep off all cowans and eavesdroppers, and to see that none pass or repass but such as are duly qualified and have permission from the Worshipful Master.

The Master then seats the Senior and Junior Deacon with one rap.

W. M. to S. W. Are you a Master Mason?

S. W. I am.

W. M. What induced you to become a Master Mason?

S. W. In order that I might receive Masters' wages, and be thereby better enabled to support myself and family, and contribute to the relief of poor, distressed Master Masons, their widows and orphans.

W. M. to S. W. Where were you made a Master Mason?

S. W. to W. M. In a just and lawfully constituted Lodge of Master Masons.

After having rehearsed as much of the lecture as he deems necessary, the Master proceeds as follows:

W. M. to S. W. How many anciently composed a Lodge of Master Masons

S. W. to W. M. Three or more.

W. M. to S. W. When composed of only three, who were they?

ENTERED APPRENTICE, OR FIRST DEGREE.

S. W. to W. M. The Worshipful Master, Senior Warden and Junior Warden.

W. M. to S. W. What is the Junior Warden's station in the Lodge?

S. W. to W. M. In the South.

W. M. Why are you in the South, Brother Junior Warden? What are your duties there?

J. W. As the Sun in the South at its meridian height is the glory and beauty of the day, so stands the Junior Warden in the South, the better to observe the time; to call the craft from labor to refreshment; to superintend them during the hours thereof, and see that they do not convert the purposes of refreshment into intemperance and excess, to call them on again in due season, that the Worshipful Master may have pleasure and the craft profit thereby.

W. M. What is the Senior Warden's station in the Lodge?

J. W. In the West.

W. M. Why are you in the West, Brother Senior Warden? What are you duties there?

S. W. As the Sun is in the West at the close of the day, so is the Senior Warden in the West to assist the Worshipful Master in opening and closing his Lodge; to pay the craft their wages, if any be due, and see that none go away dissatisfied, harmony being the strength and support of all societies, more especially of our.

W. M. What is the Worshipful Master's station in the Lodge?

S. W. In the East.

ENTERED APPRENTICE, OR FIRST DEGREE.

W. M. Why is he in the East, Brother Senior Warden? What are his duties there?

S. W. As the Sun rises in the East to open and govern the day, so rises the Worshipful Master in the East to open and govern his Lodge; to set the craft to work, and give them good and wholesome instruction for their labors.

This closes the opening lecture. The Master gives three raps, which call up the Lodge, he rising last.

W. M. Brother Senior Warden, it is my will and pleasure that ——— Lodge number——— be now opened on the third degree of Masonry, for the dispatch of such business as may regularly come before it, under the usual Masonic restrictions. Communicate this order to the Junior Warden in the South and he to the craft for their government.

S. W. to J. W. *(turning to that officer in the South.)* Brother Junior Warden, it is the will and pleasure of the Worshipful Master in the East that ——— Lodge number——— be now opened on the third degree of Masonry, for the dispatch of such business as may regularly come before it, under the usual Masonic restrictions. Communicate this order to the craft for their government.

J. W. to Lodge. Brethren, it is the will and pleasure of the Worshipful Master in the East, communicated to me by the Senior Warden in the West, that ——— Lodge number——— be now opened on the third degree of Masonry, for the dispatch of such business as may regularly come before it, under the usual Masonic restrictions. Take notice, and govern yourselves accordingly. Look to the East.

ENTERED APPRENTICE, OR FIRST DEGREE.

W. M. to Lodge. Brethren, together, and the Signs.

The craft all face towards the Worshipful Master, who makes, slowly and distinctly, the signs of an Entered Apprentice, Fellow Craft and Master Mason, successively, which are imitated simultaneously by the craft.

After the signs have been made the Junior Warden gives one rap with his gavel, followed by the Senior Warden in the West and by the Master in the East. These raps are passed thrice about the stations.

The Master now takes off his hat and says: "Let us pray."

The prayer is offered by the Master or Chaplain. After prayer the Master announces to the Lodge:

W. M. In the name of God and the Holy Saints John, I declare ―――― Lodge Number ―――― opened in form on the third degree. Brother Junior Deacon, inform the Tyler.

The Master seats the craft by one rap. The Junior Deacon goes to the door and knocks thrice upon it, on which it is opened by the Tyler, to whom the Junior Deacon announces that the Lodge is opened in the third degree. He then shuts the door, which is locked on the outside by the Tyler.

J. D. to W. M. The duty is performed, Worshipful Master.

The Master seats the Junior Deacon by one rap. While this is in progress, the Senior Deacon takes the Three Great Lights from the Secretary's table and arranges them duly upon the altar; the Bible

ENTERED APPRENTICE, OR FIRST DEGREE.

laying open at Ecclesiastes XII, and both points of the compasses above the square.

The Lesser Lights are placed in their proper position, two at the North-east and North-west corners of the altar, and the third between them, a little further Northward. The Wardens reverse their columns, erect in the West, down in the South.

As has already been stated, all matters of business are transacted in the Lodge when opened on the third degree; when the work of initiation is to be done, the Lodge must be called off in the third degree, and remain so until duly opened in the first degree; when an Entered Apprentice is to be passed, the Lodge is called off in the third degree, and remains so while the second degree is opened; if a Fellow Craft is to be raised the Lodge remains in the Master Mason's degree.

After the ceremonies of opening are concluded, the Master requests the Secretary to read the minutes of their last regular communication. This being done, the Master asks as follows:

W. M. to S. W. Brother Senior Warden, have you any alterations to propose?

If the Senior Warden has any remarks to make, he now does so, first making the sign of a Master Mason. If he has nothing to offer by way of amendment, he says:

S. W. to W. M. *(making the sign of a Master Mason.)* I have none, Worshipful Master.

W. M. to J. W. Have you any, Brother Junior Warden?

J. W. to W. M. *(making the sign.)* None. Worshipful Master.

ENTERED APPRENTICE, OR FIRST DEGREE.

W. M. to Lodge. Has any brother around the Lodge any alterations to propose?

If none are offered the Master puts the question of the adoption of the minutes, etc., and then follows the other regular business of the Lodge, viz:

2. Reading and referring petitions.
3. Reports of Committees.
4. Balloting for Candidates.
5. Conferring Degrees.
6. Unfinished business.
7. Disposing of such other business as may lawfully come before the Lodge.

When the Master announces the fifth order of business *(conferring degrees)*, he proceeds as follows:

W. M. to J. D. Brother Junior Deacon, you will ascertain whether there are any candidates in waiting, and if so, who, and for what degree.

The Junior Deacon proceeds to the preparation room, and having ascertained that a candidate is there, reports as follows:

J. D. to W. M. Worshipful Master, Mr. A. B. is in waiting for the first degree.

The seventh and last order of business includes the work of initiation, passing and raising, and when all the other business of the Lodge has been transacted, the Master proceeds as follows:

W. M. Brethren, if there is no further business before this Lodge of Master Masons, we will proceed to close, and open an Entered Apprentice Lodge for the purpose of initiation.

ENTERED APPRENTICE, OR FIRST DEGREE.

CALLING A LODGE FROM A HIGHER TO A LOWER DEGREE.

The following is a short way of calling a Lodge from a higher degree to a lower one, and is employed by Masters when pressed for time:

W. M. Brother Senior Warden, you will call the craft to order as Entered Apprentices *(or Fellow Crafts, as the case may be)*, reserving yourself for the last.

S. W. *(gives three raps and all rise to their feet.)* Brethren, you will come to order as Entered Apprentice Masons.

The proper signs are now given, and the Junior Warden gives one rap in the South; the Senior Warden one rap in the West and the Master one rap in the East.

W. M. I now declare this Lodge opened in the first degree of Masonry for the dispatch of business. Brother Junior Deacon, you will inform the Tyler. Brother Senior Deacon, attend to the altar.

The foregoing way of lowering a Lodge has the merit of saving time, but the proper and more beautiful method is as follows:

W. M. Brother Junior Warden, how goes the hour?

J. W. It is now high twelve, Worshipful Master.

W. M. It being high twelve, you will call the craft from labor to refreshment for the purpose of opening a Lodge of Entered Apprentices.

J. W. *(calls up the Lodge with three raps.)* Brethren, it is the will and pleasure of the Worship-

ENTERED APPRENTICE, OR FIRST DEGREE.

ful Master in the East, that the Lodge be now called from labor to refreshments for the purpose of opening a Lodge of Entered Apprentices; take notice and govern yourselves accordingly.—Look to the East!

W. M. Brethren, we are at refreshments. Brother Junior Deacon, inform the Tyler. Brother Senior Deacon, arrange the three Great Lights.

The three Great Lights are closed. The Wardens reverse their columns, erect in the South, down in the East.

OPENING A LODGE OF ENTERED APPRENTICES.

W. M. Brother Senior Warden, proceed to satisfy yourself that all present are Entered Apprentices.

S. W. All present are Entered Apprentices.

The Master calls up the Senior and Junior Deacons by one rap.

W. M. to J. D. Brother Junior Deacon, what is the first great care of Masons when in Lodge assembled?

J. D. To see that the Lodge is duly tyled, Worshipful Master.

W. M. Perform that duty, inform the Tyler that I am about to open a Lodge of Entered Apprentices, and direct him to tyle accordingly.

The Junior Deacon then goes to the door, opens it, and finding the Tyler stationed outside, duly armed, he informs him of the Master's order and shuts the door.

J. D. The Lodge is duly tyled, Worshpful Master.

ENTERED APPRENTICE, OR FIRST DEGREE.

W. M. How are we tyled, Brother Junior Deacon?

J. D. By a brother Master Mason without the door, armed with the proper instrument of his office.

W. M. What are his duties there?

J. D. To keep off all cowans and eavesdroppers, and to see that none pass or repass but such as are duly qualified and have permission from the Worshipful Master. *(Master now gives one rap and seats the Deacons.)*

W. M. to S. W. Brother Senior Warden, as an Entered Apprentice, from whence came you?

S. W. From the Lodge of the Holy Saints John at Jerusalem.

W. M. What came you here to do?

S. W. To learn to subdue my passions and improve myself in masonry.

W. M. Then I presume you are a Mason?

S. W. I am so taken and accepted among brothers and fellows.

W. M. What makes you a Mason.

S. W. My obligation.

W. M. How do you know yourself to be a Mason?

S. W. By having been often tried, never denied, and am willing to be tried again.

W. M. How shall I know you to be a Mason?

S. W. By certain signs, a token, a word, and the perfect points of my entrance.

After proceeding with such further portion of the lecture as he may see fit, the Master continues as follows:

W. M. Where were you made an Entered Apprentice?

ENTERED APPRENTICE, OR FIRST DEGREE.

S. W. In a just and lawfully constituted Lodge of Entered Apprentices.

W. M. How many anciently composed a Lodge of Entered Apprentices?

S. W. Seven or more.

W. M. When composed of only seven, who were they?

S. W. The Worshipful Master, Senior Warden, Junior Warden, Treasurer, Secretary, Senior Deacon and Junior Deacon.

W. M. What is the Junior Deacon's place in the Lodge?

S. W. On the right of the Senior Warden, in the West.

W. M. What are your duties there, Brother Junior Deacon?

J. D. To carry messages from the Senior Warden in the West to the Junior Warden in the South, and elsewhere about the Lodge, as he may direct, and to see that the Lodge is duly tyled.

W. M. What is the Senior Deacon's place in the Lodge?

J. D. On the right of the Worshipful Master, in the East.

W. M. What are your duties there, Brother Senior Deacon?

S. D. To carry orders from the Worshipful Master in the East to the Senior Warden in the West, and elsewhere about the Lodge, as he may direct; to welcome and accommodate visiting brethren; to receive and conduct candidates.

W. M. What is the Secretary's place in the Lodge?

ENTERED APPRENTICE, OR FIRST DEGREE.

S. D. To the left of the Worshipful Master in the East. (Here the Master calls up the Secretary, Treasurer and Junior and Senior Wardens by two raps.)

W. M. What are your duties there, Brother Secretary?

Sec. To observe the Worshipful Master's will and pleasure; to record the proceedings of the Lodge, to receive all moneys and to pay them into the hands of the Treasurer.

W. M. What is the Treasurer's place in the Lodge?

Sec. On the right of the Worshipful Master, in the East.

W. M. What are you duties there, Brother Treasurer?

Treas. To receive all moneys from the hand of the Secretary; keep just and regular account of the same, and pay them out at the Worshipful Master's will and pleasure, with the consent of the Lodge.

W. M. What is the Junior Warden's station in the Lodge?

Treas. In the South.

W. M. Why are you in the South, Brother Junior Warden? What are you duties there?

J. W. As the Sun in the South at its meridian height is the glory and beauty of the day, so stands the Junior Warden in the South, the better to observe the time to call the craft from labor to refreshment, to superintend them during the hours thereof, and see that they do not convert the purposes of refreshment into intemperance and excess; to call

ENTERED APPRENTICE, OR FIRST DEGREE.

them on again in due season, that the Worshipful Master may have pleasure and the craft profit thereby.

W. M. What is the Senior Warden's station in the Lodge?

J. W. In the West.

W. M. Why are you in the West, Brother Senior Warden? What are your duties there?

S. W. As the Sun is in the West at the close of the day, so is the Senior Warden in the West, to assist the Worshipful Master in opening and closing his Lodge; to pay the craft their wages, if any be due, and see that none go away dissatisfied, harmony being the strength and support of all societies, more especially of ours.

W. M. What is the Worshipful Master's station in the Lodge?

S. W. In the East.

W. M. Why is he in the East, Brother Senior Warden? What are his duties there?

S. W. As the Sun rises in the East to open and govern the day, so rises the Worshipful Master in the East to open and govern his Lodge; to set the craft to work, and give them good and wholesome instruction for their labors.

The Master now calls up the Lodge by three raps, himself rising last.

W. M. Brother Senior Warden, it is my will and pleasure that ——— Lodge number ——— be now opened on the first degree of Masonry for the dispatch of such business as may regularly come before it, under the usual Masonic restrictions. Communi-

ENTERED APPRENTICE, OR FIRST DEGREE.

cate this order to the Junior Warden in the South, and he to the craft for their government.

S. W. to J. W. *(turning to that officer in the South.)* Brother Junior Warden, it is the will and pleasure of the Worshipful Master in the East that ——— Lodge number ——— be now opened on the first degree of Masonry, for the dispatch of such business as may regularly come before it, under the usual Masonic restrictions. Communicate this order to the craft for their government.

J. W. to Lodge. Brethren, it is the will and pleasure of the Worshipful Master in the East, communicated to be by the Senior Warden in the West, that ——— Lodge number ——— be now opened on the first degree of Masonry, for the dispatch of such business as may regularly come before it, under the usual Masonic restrictions. Take notice and govern yourselves accordingly.—Look to the East!

The craft now face the Master, and with him make, clowly and carefully, the signs of an Entered Apprentice.

After the signs are given, the Junior Warden in the South gives one rap, followed by the Senior Warden in the West and the Worshipful Master in the East.

After the usual prayer, the Master proceeds:—

W. M. to Lodge. In the name of God, and the Holy Saints John, I declare ——— Lodge number ——— opened in form on the first degree. Brother Junior Deacon, inform the Tyler.

The Master seats the Lodge by one rap.

The Junior Deacon repairs to the door and knocks

ENTERED APPRENTICE, OR FIRST DEGREE.

thrice upon it, when it is opened by the Tyler, to whom the Junior Deacon announces that the Lodge is opened upon the first degree. He then shuts the door and the Tyler locks it upon the outside.

J. D. to W. M. The duty is performed, Worshipful Master.

The Master seats the Deacon by one rap.

Meanwhile, the Senior Deacon arranges the three Great Lights duly upon the altar, the Bible laying open at Psalm CXXXIII, and both points of the compasses are laid underneath the square. The Wardens reverse their columns, erect in the West, down in the South.

CEREMONIES OF INITIATION.

W. M. Brother Stewards, you will repair to the preparation room, where you will find a candidate in waiting, whom you will duly prepare for the first degree of Masonry. (Before the Stewards leave the Lodge room, they step to the altar and make the proper sign. Leaving the altar on their right they proceed to the preparation room.)

After the candidate has responded to the usual questions, and has been properly prepared for initiation by the Stewards, he is conducted to the door and requested to give three distinct knows.

S. D. to W. M. *(risng and making signs.)* There is an alarm at the door of the preparation room.

W. M. Attend to the alarm.

The Senior Deacon, leaving the altar on his right, goes to the door, and answers the alarm by three similar knocks. The door is then partially opened.

ENTERED APPRENTICE, OR FIRST DEGREE.

S. D. Who comes here?

Steward. A poor, blind candidate, who is desirous of being brought from darkness to light, and receiving a part of the rights, lights and benefits of this Worshipful Lodge erected to God and dedicated to the Holy Saints John, as many a brother and fellow has done before him.

S. D. to Candidate. Is it of your own free will and accord.

Candidate. It is.

S. D. to Steward. Is he duly and truly prepared?

Steward. He is.

S. D. Is he worthy and well qualified?

Steward. He is.

S. D. By what further right or benefit does he expect to gain admission?

Steward. By being a man, free born, of lawful age and well recommended.

S. D. Let him wait with patience until the Worshipful Master is informed of his request, and his answer returned.

The Senior Deacon closes the door, goes to the altar, salutes the Master, and gives three distinct raps on the floor with his rod.

W. M. Who comes there?

S. D. A poor, blind candidate, who is desirous of being brought from darkness to light, and receiving a part of the rights, lights and benefits of this Worshipful Lodge erected to God and dedicated to the Holy Saints John, as many a brother and fellow has done before him.

W. M. Is it of his own free will and accord?

ENTERED APPRENTICE, OR FIRST DEGREE.

S. D. It is.

W. M. Is he duly and truly prepared?

S. D. He is.

W. M. Is he worthy and well qualified?

S. D. He is.

W. M. By what further right or benefit does he expect to gain admission?

S. D. By being a man, free born, of lawful age and well recommended.

W. M. Since he comes endowed with all these essential qualifications, it is my will and pleasure that he enter this Lodge of Entered Apprentices, and that you receive him in due and ancient form.

The Senior Deacon repairs to the door, opens it wide and says:

S. D. to Stewards. It is the will and pleasure of the Worshipful Master that the poor bling candidate enter this Lodge of Entered Apprentices.

The two Stewards conduct the candidate into the Lodge, close the door and take their seats.

The Senior Deacon places his left hand on the right shoulder of candidate, and says:

S. D. to Candidate. My friend, it is the will and pleasure of the Worshipful Master that I receive you into this Lodge of Entered Apprentices in due and ancient form. I place this sharp instrument *(jewel of office)* at your naked left breast. It is to show that as this is an instrument of torture to the flesh, so shall the remembrance thereof be to your conscience, should you ever presume to reveal any of the secrets of Masonry unlawfully.

The Senior Deacon now takes the candidate by the left arm and the Worshipful Master says:

ENTERED APPRENTICE, OR FIRST DEGREE.

W. M. to Candidate. My friends, no man should ever enter upon any great and important undertaking without first invoking the blessing of Deity. You will be conducted to the centre of the Lodge, and caused to kneel and attend prayer.

The Master calls up the Lodge by three raps, himself rising last, uncovers his head and repeats the following prayer in the East: Vouchsafe thine aid, Almighty Father of the Universe, to this our present convention; and grant that this candidate for Masonry may dedicate and devote his life to thy service, and become a true and faithful brother among us! Endue him with a competency of thy Divine wisdom, that, by the secrets of our art, he may be better enabled to display the beauties of Brotherly love, Relief and Truth, to the honor of thy holy name. *Amen. So mote it be.*

After the prayer the Worshipful Master goes to the candidate, places his right hand upon his head, and says:

W. M. to Candidate. In whom do you put your trust?

Candidate. In God.

W. M. Your trust being in God, your faith is well founded, arise! *(takes him by the right arm and assists him to rise)* follow your guide, and fear no danger.

The Worshipful Master returns to the East, seats himself and the Lodge by one rap.

The Senior Deacon now takes the candidate's left hand in his own right hand, using the appropriate grip, and leads him with slow and measured steps in

ENTERED APPRENTICE, OR FIRST DEGREE.

a direct line near the N. E. corner of the Lodge; thence making a right angle to the S. E. corner; thence to the S. W. corner; thence to the N. W. corner, and so regularly about the Lodge; finally, in front of the Junior Warden's station in the South and one pace distant, when he halts and faces the Junior Warden. As they pass the Junior Warden's station the first time, that officer gives one rap. Instantly the Worshipful Master begins to read from the 133d Psalm as follows: "Behold, how good, and how pleasant it is for brethren to dwell together in unity. It is like the precious ointment on the head, that ran down upon the beard, even Aaron's beard, that went down to the skirts of his garments; as the dew of Hermon, and as the dew that descended upon the mountains of Zion; for there the Lord commanded the blessing, even life for evermore." The reading is timed so accruately that the Psalm is completed just as the candidate and his conductor finish the circuit of the Lodge, and arrive at the Junior Warden's station in the South. As they pass the Senior Warden's station in the West, that officer gives one rap, and the Worshipful Master signifies the passage of his station by one rap.

Having halted, as described, before the Junior Warden, the Senior Deacon gives three raps on the floor with his rod.

J. W. to S. D. Who comes here?

S. D. A poor blind candidate who is desirous of being brought from darkness to light, and receiving a part in the rights, lights and benefits of this Worshipful Lodge erected to God, and dedicated to the

ENTERED APPRENTICE, OR FIRST DEGREE.

Holy Saints John, as many a brother and fellow has done before him.

J. W. to Candidate. Is it of your own free will and accord?

Candidate. It is.

J. W. to S. D. Is he duly and truly prepared?

S. D. He is.

J. W. Is he worthy and well qualified?

S. D. He is.

J. W. By what further right or benefit does he expect to gain admission?

S. D. By being a man, free born, of lawful age and well recommended.

J. W. to S. D. Conduct the candidate to the Senior Warden in the West for further examination.

The Senior Deacon now conducts the candidate in front of the Senior Warden's station in the West, halts one pace distant, faces that officer, and gives three raps on the floor with his rod.

The same question are asked and like answers returned as at the Junior Warden's station.

S. W. to S. D. Conduct the candidate to the Worshipful Master in the East for final examination.

The Senior Deacon conducts the candidate to the Worshipful Master's station in the East, where the three knocks are given, the same questions asked and like answers returned, as before.

W. M. to Candidate. You will be reconducted to the Senior Warden in the West, who will teach you to approach towards the East, advancing by one upright, regular step, your feet forming the right angle of an oblong square, your body erect to the Worshipful Master in the East.

ENTERED APPRENTICE, OR FIRST DEGREE.

The Senior Deacon obeys the order, taking care to leave the altar on the right.

S. D. to S. W. It is the will and pleasure of the Worshipful Master in the East that this candidate be taught to approach to the East, advancing by one upright, regular step, his feet forming the right angle of an oblong square, his body erect to the Worshipful Master in the East.

S. W. to S. D. You will see that the Worshipful Master's orders are obeyed.

The Senior Deacon now causes the candidate to face to the East, and instructs him how to take the proper step as follows:

S. D. to Candidate. You will face to the East. Step off with your left foot, bring the heel of the right foot to the hollow of the left foot, and form the right angle of an oblong square. Stand erect!

S. D. to W. M. Your orders have been obeyed, Worshipful Master.

While the candidate is in this position, the Worshipful Master (who does not leave his seat) addresses him as follows:

W. M. My friend, for the first time in your life you have advance to the altar of Masonry. You stand before us a candidate seeking admission into our order. But, before going further, be warned of the solemnity and importance of the step you are about to take; and, if unwilling to proceed, withdraw while there is yet time.

The design of the Masonic Institution is to make its votaries wiser, better, and consequently happier. We receive none knowingly into our ranks who are

ENTERED APPRENTICE, OR FIRST DEGREE.

not moral and upright before God, and of good repute before the world. Such persons, when associated together, will naturally seek each other's welfare and happiness equally with their own. That they may do so upon a common platform, and become not weary in well doing, we obligate them by solemn and irrevocable ties to perform the requirements of, and avoid the things prohibted by Masonry. You have been elected by the members of this Lodge, upon your own voluntary petition, to become united with use in this great and good work. At your entrance into the Lodge, you professed faith in God; that God whom we, as Masons, reverence and serve. The solemn engagements which you will be required to make before you can participate in our labors and privileges are made in the name of God, and when once taken they can never be repudiated or laid aside. Yet, I am free to inform you that our obligation contains nothing which can conflct with your duty to God, your country, your neighbor or yourself.

With this pledge on my part, as the Master of the Lodge, I ask you, are you willing to take such an obligation, as all Masons have done before you; or do you prefer to retire, as you have a perfect right to do, and proceed no further?

If the candidate consents to take the obligation, the Master orders as follows:

W. M. to S. D. Place the candidate in due form to be made a Mason.

S. D. to Candidate. Advance! kneel on your naked left knee, place your right knee so as to form a

ENTERED APPRENTICE, OR FIRST DEGREE.

square, your body erect, your naked left hand supporting the Holy Bible, square and compasses; your naked right hand resting thereon. *(The Senior Deacon assists candidate to do this.)*

S. D. to W. M. The candidate is in due form, Worshipful Master.

The Worshipful Master calls up the Lodge by three raps; he rises last, uncovers his head, goes to and stands erect before the altor, and places his right hand upon the Bible. The Senior Deacon takes a positon behind the candidate.

W. M. to Candidate. You will repeat your name, and say after me:

I, A. B., of my own free will and accord, in the presence of Almighty God, and this Worshipful Lodge erected to Him and dedicated to the Holy Saints John, do hereby and hereon (Master presses his gravel on candidate's knuckles) most solemnly and sincerely promises and swear that I will always *hail*, forever conceal, never reveal any of the secret arts, parts or points of the hidden mysteries of Masonry which may have been heretofore, or shall be, at this time, or at any future period, communicated to me as such,: to any person or persons, whomsoever, except it be a true and lawful brother Mason, or within the body of a just and lawfully constituted Lodge of Masons; nor unto him or them until, by strict trial, due examination, or lawful information, I shall have found him, or them, as lawfully entitled to them as I am myself. I furthermore promise and swear that I will not write, print, paint, stamp, stain, cut, carve, show, mark, or engrave them on

ENTERED APPRENTICE, OR FIRST DEGREE.

any thing movable or immovable capable of receiving the least impression of a sign, word, syllable, letter or character, whereby they may become legible or intelligible to any person under the canopy of heaven, and the secrets of Masonry be thereby unlawfully obtained by my unworthiness.

All this I most solemnly and sincerely promise and swear, with a firm and steadfast resolution to keep and perform the same, without the least equivocation, mental reservation or secret evasion whatsoever; binding myself under no less penalty than that of having my throat cut from ear to ear, my tongue torn out by its roots, and buried in the sands of the sea, at low-water mark, where the tide ebbs and flows twice in twenty-four hours, should I, in the least, knowingly or wittingly violate or transgress this my Entered Apprentice obligation. So help me God, and keep me steadfast.

W. M. to Candidate. In token of your sincerity of purpose in this solemn engagement, you will kiss the Holy Bible, now open before you.

The candidate kisses the Bible.

W. M. to S. D. Brother Senior Deacon, our brother being now bound to use by a covenant which connot be broken, you will release him from his cable tow.

The order is obeyed.

W. M. to Candidate. My brother, for by that sacred appellation I now address you, in your present blind condition what do you most desire?

Candidate *(prompted by the Senior Deacon.)* Light.

W. M. Light being your desire, you will receive

ENTERED APPRENTICE, OR FIRST DEGREE.

it. *(To the Lodge.)* My brethren, assist me in bringing our brother to light.

The brethren all (except the Wardens) come forward and form themselves in two parallel lines from East to West.

Wm. M. "In the beginning God created the heavens and the earth. And the earth was without from and void; and darkness was upon the face of the deep. And the spirt of God moved upon the face of the waters. And God said, let there be light, and there was light." In solemn commemoration of that sublime event, I, in like manner, Masonically declare, let there be light!

At the word *light*, all present strike their hands together once, and stamp with their right feet. The Senior Deacon removes the hoodwink at the same instant, and the Worshipful Master declares: And there is light!

W. M. to Candidate. Upon being brought to Masonic light, you behold upon the altar before you the three Great Lights of Masonry—the Holy Bible square and compasses, by the light of the three Lesser Lights, of which these three burning tapers, placed in a triangular position, are the representatives. The Holy Boble is the rule and guide of Faith; the square, to square our actions, and the compasses to circumscribe and keep us within due bounds with all mankind, but more especially with a brother Mason. The three Lesser Lights are the sun, moon and Master of the Lodge, and are thus expained: As the sun rules the day and the moon governs the night, so ought the Worshipful Master

ENTERED APPRENTICE, OR FIRST DEGREE.

to endeavor to rule and givern his Lodge with equal regularity.

The Master now retires to the East and advancing, says:

W. M. to Candidate. You now discover me approaching you from the East under the due guard *(makes due guard)* aud sign *(makes sign)* of an Entered Apprentice. In token of my brother love and favor I present you with my right hand *(takes candidate, who is yet kneeling at the altar, by the right hand)*, and with the grip and word of an Entered Apprentice. Arise and salute the Wardens as an Entered Apprentice.

The Master retires to his station, seats himself, and then seats the Lodge by one rap.

The Senior Deacon conducts the candidate to the Junior Warden's station in the South, leaving the altar on the right, when the candidate salutes the Junior Warden with the due guard and sign of an Entered Apprentice. They then pass on to the Senior Warden's station and salute the Senior Warden in the same manner. Then they go to the West of the altar and salute the Worshipful Master.

The Master now takes an apron in his hand, and calls up the Lodge by three raps, himself rising last, and goes to candidate.

W. M. to Candidate. My brother, I now present you with the lamb-skin or white leather apron. It is an emblem of innocence and the badge of a Mason. It is more ancient than the Golden Fleece or Roman Eagle, more honorable than the Star and Garter, or any other order that can be conferred

ENTERED APPRENTICE, OR FIRST DEGREE.

upon you at this time, or at any furture period, by kings, princes, potentates, or any other person, except he be a Mason. I hope you will wear it with equal pleasure to yourself and honor to the fraternity. Take it, carry it to the Senior Warden in the West; he will teach you how to wear it as an Entered Apprentice.

The Master returns to the East and seats the Lodge with one rap. The Senior Deacon conducts the candidate to the Senior Warden in the West and says:

S. D. Brother Senior Warden, it is the will and pleasure of the Worshipful Master in the East that our newly admitted brother be taught how to wear his apron as an Entered Apprentice.

S. W. to Candidate. My brother, at the building of King Solomon's Temple there were three principal classes of Masons, and each, as a distinctive badge, wore his apron in a peculiar manner. Entered Apprentices being the bearers of burthens, were directed to wear theirs with the bib turned up, so as to protect their clothing. Thus, my brother, will you wear yours while laboring among us as a speculative Entered Apprentice. But remember that, although stains upon this garment brought credit rather than disgrace to the Ancient Entered Apprentice, you, as a speculative Entered Apprentice, must keep this apron, as an emblem of innocense, unspotted before the world.

The candidate is invested by the Senior Deacon, who now conducts him back to the West of the altar and they salute the Worshipful Master.

ENTERED APPRENTICE, OR FIRST DEGREE.

S. D. to W. M: Your orders have been obeyed, Worshipful Master.

W. M. to Candidate. My brother, agreeable to an ancient custom in all regular and well-governed Lodges, it is now necessary that you be required to deposit something of a metallic kind, not for its intrinsic worth or value, but that it may be laid up among the relics in the archives of this Lodge, as a memorial that you are now made a Mason. Examine yourself strictly and see if you can find such an object.

Candidate *(prompted by S. D.)* I find myself entirely destitute, Worshipful Master.

W. M. to Candidate. This requirement was to remind you of your now extremely poor and penniless situation. Should you ever afterwards meet a friend, more especially a brother, in like condition, you must contribute as liberally to his relief as you can do without inconvenience to yourself. You will now be reconducted to the place from when you came, there be re-invested of what you were divested, and return to the Lodge for further instruction.

The Senior Deacon conducts the candidate to the altar, they salute the Worshipful Master and then go to the preparation room, where the Senior Deacon places the candidate in charge of the Stewards and returns to his place in the Lodge. When the candidate is re-invested, the Stewards bring him back into the Lodge and the Senior Deacon again takes charge of him. The Stewards then go to the altar, salute the Master and take their seats. The

ENTERED APPRENTICE, OR FIRST DEGREE.

Senior Deacon conducts the candidate to the altar where they salute the Master.

W. M. to Candidate. My brother, you will now be placed in the North-east corner of the Lodge, as the youngest Entered Apprentice; form with your feet the right angle of an oblong square. Stand with your body erect to the East. *(The Senior Deacon assists him to do this.)* Now, my brother, you stand as a just and upright Mason, and I give it you strictly in charge ever to walk and act as such. The Master now calls up the Lodge with three raps, rising last himself, and delivers the charge.

Brother: As you are now introduced into the first principles of Masonry, I congratulate you on being accepted into this ancient and honorable order; ancient, as having subsisted from time immemorial; and honorable, as tending in every particular so to render all men who will be conformable to its precepts. No institution was ever raised on a better principle or more solid foundation; nor were ever more excellent rules and useful maxims laid down than are inculcated in the several Masonic lectures. The greatest and best of men in all ages have been encouragers and promoters of the art, and have never deemed it derogatory from their dignity to level themselves with the fraternity, extend their privileges and patronize their assemblies.

There are *three great duties* which, as a Mason, you are charged to inculcate—to God, your neighbor and yourself. To God, in never mentioning His name but with that reverental awe which is due

ENTERED APPRENTICE, OR FIRST DEGREE.

from a creature to his Creator; to implore His aid in all your laudable undertakings, and to esteem Him as the chief good. To your neighbor, in acting upon the square, and doing unto him as you wish he should do unto you; and to yourself, in avoiding all irregularity and intemperance, which may impair your faculties or debase the dignity of your profession. A zealous attachement to these duties will insure public and private esteem.

In the State you are to be a quiet and peaceable citizen, true to your government and just to your country; you are not to countenance disloyalty or rebellion, but patiently submit to legal authority, and conform with cheerfulness to the government of the country in which you live.

In your outward demeanor be particularly careful to avoid censure or reproach. Let not interest, favor or prejudice bias your integrity or influence you to be guilty of a dishonorable action. Although your frequent appearance at our regular meetings is earnestly solicited, yet it is not meant that Masonry should interfere with your necessary vocations, for these are on no account to be neglected; neither are you to suffer your zeal for the institution to lead you into arguments with those who, through ignorance, may ridicule it. At your leisure hours, that you may improve in Masonic knowledge, you are to converse with well-informed brethren, who will be always as ready to give as you will be ready to receive instruction.

Finally, keep sacred and inviolable the mysteries of the order, as these are to distinguish you from

ENTERED APPRENTICE, OR FIRST DEGREE.

the rest of the community, and mark your consequence among Masons. If, in the circle of your acquaintance, you find a person desirious of being initiated into Masonry, be particularly attentive not to recommend him unless you are convinced he will conform to our rules, that the honor, glory and reputation of the institution may be firmly established, and the world at large convinced of its good effects.

After the charge is delivered, the Master seats the Lodge by one rap.

W. M. to Candidate. I now present you with the working tools of an Entered Apprentice, and will teach you their uses. The working tools of an Entered Apprentice are the twenty-four inch gauge and the common gavel.

The twenty-our inch gauge is an instrument made use of by operative masons to measure and lay out their work; but we, as Free and Accepted Masons, are taught to make use of it for the more noble and glorious purpose of dividing our time. It being divided into twenty-four equal parts, is emblematical of the twenty-four hours of the day, which we are taught to divide into three equal parts, whereby we find eight hours for the service of God and a distressed worthy brother, eight hours for our usual avocations, and eight hours for refreshment and sleep.

The common gavel is an instrument made use of by operative masons to break off the corners of rough stones, the better to fit them for the builder's use; but we, as Free and Accepted Masons, are taught to make use of it for the more noble and glo-

ENTERED APPRENTICE, OR FIRST DEGREE.

rious purpose of divesting our minds and consciences of all the vices and superfluities of life, thereby fitting our bodies as living stones for that spiritual building, that house not made with hands, eternal in the heavens.

W. M. to Candidate. You will now seated.

The Senior Deacon seats candidate in a chair in front of the Worshipful Master in the East, and between him and the altar.

The Master, with the assistance of the Senior Warden or some other well-informed brother, rehearses the three sections of the Entered Apprentice Lecture; after which the candidate is seated.

ENTERED APPRENTICE LECTURE.

SECTION FIRST.

W. M. As an Entered Apprentice, from whence come you?

S. W. From the Lodge of the Holy Saints John at Jerusalem.

W. M. What come you here to do?

S. W. To learn to subdue my passions and improve myself in Masonry.

W. M. Then I presume you are a Mason.

S. W. I am so taken and accepted among brothers and fellows.

W. M. What makes you a Mason?

S. W. My obligation.

W. M. How do you know yourself to be a Mason?

S. W. By having been often tried and never denied, and am willing to be tried again.

ENTERED APPRENTICE, OR FIRST DEGREE.

W. M. How shall I know you to be a Mason?

S. W. By certain signs, a token, a word, and the perfect points of my entrance.

W. M. What are signs?

S. W. Right angles, horizontals and perpendiculars.

W. M. What is a token?

S. W. A certain friendly and brotherly grip whereby one Mason may know another in the dark as well as the light.

W. M. Give me a sign. *(Gives sign.)*

W. M. Hast that an allusion?

S. W. It has; to the penalty of my obligation.

W. M. *(Taking S. W. by right hand as in ordinary hand shaking.)* Give me a token? I hail.

S. W. I conceal.

W. M. What do you conceal?

S. W. All the secrets of Masons in Masonry to which this token alludes. *(At the word "token" the grips performed.)*

S. W. I conceal.

W. M. What is that?

S. W. The grip of an Entered Apprentice.

Here follow five questions and answers which refer solely to certain landmarks.

W. M. Where were you first prepared to be made a Mason?

S. W. In my heart.

W. M. Where next?

S. W. In a room adjacent to a just and lawfully constituted Lodge of Masons.

W. M. How were you prepared?

S. W. By being divested of all metals, neither

ENTERED APPRENTICE, OR FIRST DEGREE.

naked nor clothed, barefoot nor shod, hoodwinked, and a cable-tow about my neck; in which situation I was conducted to the door of the Lodge by a friend, whom I afterward found to be a brother.

W. M. How did you know it to be a door, being hoodwinked?

S. W. By first meeting resistance and afterwards gaining admission.

W. M. How gained you admission?

S. W. By three knocks.

W. M. What was said to you from within?

S. W. Who comes here?

W. M. Your answer?

S. W. A poor, blind candidate, who is desirous of being brought from darkness to light, and receiving a part of the rights, lights and benefits of this Worshipful Lodge, erected to God and dedicated to the Holy Saints John, as many a brother and fellow has done before him.

W. M. What were you then asked?

S. W. If it was of my own free will and accord; if I was duly and truly prepared; worth and well qualified. All of which being answered in the affirmative, I was asked by what further right or benefit I expected to gain admission.

W. M. Your answer?

S. W. By being a man, free born, of lawful age and well recommended.

W. M. What follow?

S. W. I was directed to wait with patience until the Worshipful Master was informed of my request and his answer returned.

ENTERED APPRENTICE, OR FIRST DEGREE.

W. M. What answer did he return?

S. W. Let him enter and be received in due form.

W. M. How were you received?

S. W. On the point of a sharp instrument at my naked left breast.

W. M. How were you then disposed of?

S. W. I was conducted to the centre of the Lodge, and caused to kneel and attend prayer.

W. M. After attending prayer, what was then said to you?

S. W. In whom do you put your trust?

W. M. Your answer?

S. W. In God.

W. M. What followed?

S. W. My trust being in God, my faith was well founded. I was then taken by the right hand, ordered to arise, follow my guide and fear no danger.

W. M. Where did you follow your guide?

S. W. Once about the altar to the Junior Warden in the South, where the same question were asked and like answers returned as at the door.

W. M. How did the Junior Warden dispose of you?

S. W. He directed me to the Senior Warden in the West, where the same questions were asked and like answers returned as before.

W. M. How did the Senior Warden dispose of you?

S. W. He directed me to the Worshipful Master in the East, where the same questions were asked and like answers returned as before.

W. M. How did the Worshipful Master dispose of you?

S. W. He ordered me to be reconducted to the

ENTERED APPRENTICE, OR FIRST DEGREE.

Senior Warden in the West, who taught me to approach to the East, advancing by one upright, regular step, my feet forming the right angle of an oblong square, my body erect to the Worshipful Master in the East.

W. M. What did the Worshipful Master then do with you?

S. W. He made me a Mason.

W. M. How?

S. W. In due form.

W. M. What is that due form?

S. W. Kneeling on my naked left knee, my right forming a square, by body erect, my naked left hand supporting the Holy Bible, square and compasses, my naked right resting thereon, in which due form I took the obligation of an Entered Apprentice.

W. M. Repeat it.

S. W. Repeats the obligation. (*(For which see page 30.)*

W. M. After taking the obligation, what were you then asked?

S. W. What I most desired.

W. M. Your answer?

S. W. Light.

W. M. Did you receive it?

S. W. I did.

W. M. How?

S. W. By order of the Worshipful Master and assistance of the brethren.

W. M. On being brought to light, what did you first discover?

ENTERED APPRENTICE, OR FIRST DEGREE.

S. W. The three Great Lights of Masonry, by the light of the three lesser.

W. M. What are the three Great Lights of Masonry?

S. W. The Holy Bible, square and compasses.

W. M. What do they Masonically teach?

S. W. The Holy Bible is the rule and guide of faith; the square, to square our actions; and the compasses, to circumscribe and keep us within due bounds with all mankind, but more especially with a brother Mason.

W. M. What are the three Lesser Lights?

S. W. The Sun, Moon and Master of the Lodge.

W. M. How are they explained as such?

S. W. As the Sun rules the day and the Moon governs the night, so ought the Worshipful Master to rule and govern his Lodge with equal regularity.

W. M. How are they represented?

S. W. By three burning tapers placed in a triangular position in the Lodge.

W. M. What did you then discover?

S. W. The Worshipful Master approaching me from the East, under the due guard and sign of an Entered Apprentice; who, in token of his brotherly love and friendship, presented me with his right hand, and with it the grip and word of an Entered Apprentice, and bid me arise and salute the Wardens as such.

W. M. After saluting the Wardens, what did you then discover?

S. W. The Worshipful Master approaching me from the East a second time, who presented me with

ENTERED APPRENTICE, OR FIRST DEGREE.

the lamb-skin or white leather apron, and informed me that it was an emblem of innocence and the badge of a Mason; more ancient than the Golden Fleece or Roman Eagle; more honorable than the Star and Garter, or any other order that could be conferred on me at that time or at any future period by king, prince, potentate, or any other person, except he be a Mason; and which he hoped I would wear with equal pleasure to myself and honor to the fraternity; and bade me carry it to the Senior Warden in the West, who taught me how to wear it as an Entered Apprentice.

W. M. After being taught to wear your apron as an Entered Apprentice, what were you then informed?

S. W. That, agreeable to an ancient custom in all regular and well-governed lodges, it was then necessary that I should be required to deposit something of a metallic kind, not for its intrinsic worth or value, but that it might be laid up among the relics in the archives of the Lodge as a memorial that I was therein made a Mason, but, upon strict examination, I found myself entirely destitute.

W. M. How were you then disposed of?

S. W. I was ordered to be reconducted to the place from whence I came, there be re-invested of what I had been divested, and return to the Lodge for further instruction.

W. M. On your return to the Lodge, where were you placed, as the youngest Entered Apprentice?

S. W. In the North-east corner, my feet forming the right angle of an oblong square, my body erect,

ENTERED APPRENTICE, OR FIRST DEGREE.

to the Worshipful Master in the East, who was pleased to say that I then stood as a just and upright Mason, and gave it me strictly in charge ever to walk and act as such.

W. M. What did the Worshipful Master then present you with?

S. W. The working tools of an Entered Apprentice, and taught me their uses.

W. M. What are the working tools of an Entered Apprentice?

S. W. The twenty-four inch gauge and the common gavel.

W. M. What are their uses?

S. W. The twenty-four inch gauge is an instrument made use of by operative masons to measure and lay out their work; but we, as Free and Accepted Masons, are taught to make use of it for the more noble and glorious purpose of dividing our time. It being divided into twenty-four equal parts is emblematical of the twenty-four hours of the day, which we are taught to divide into three equal parts, whereby we find eight hours for the service of God and a distressed worthy brother, eight hours for our usual avocations, and eight hours for refreshment and sleep.

The common gavel is an instrument made use of by operative Masons to break off the corners of rough stones, the better to fit them for the build's use; but we, as Free and Accepted Masons, are taught to make use of it for the more noble and glorious purpose of divesting our minds and consciences of all the vices and superfluities of life,

ENTERED APPRENTICE, OR FIRST DEGREE.

thereby fitting our bodies as living stones of that spiritual building, that house not made with hands, eternal in the heavens.

SECTION SECOND.

W. M. Why were you divested of all metals when made a Mason?

S. W. For two reasons: first, that I should carry nothing offensive or defensive into the Lodge with me; second, at the beginning of King Solomon's temple, there was not heard the sound of axe, hammer, or any tool of iron.

W. M. How could a building of such stupendous magnitude be erected without the aid of some iron tools?

S. W. Because the stones were all hewn, squared and numbered in the quarries where they were raised; the timbers felled and prepared in the forests of Lebanon, carried by sea in floats to Joppa, and from thence by land to Jerusalem, where they were set up by wooden mauls prepared for that purpose; and when the building was erected, its several parts fitted with such exactness, that it had more the appearance of being the handiwork of the Supreme Architect of the Universe than of that of human hands.

W. M. Why were you neither naked nor clothed?

S. W. Because Masonry regards no man for his worldy wealth or honors; it was, therefore, to show that it was the internal and not the external qualifications of a man that should render him worthy to be made a Mason.

ENTERED APPRENTICE, OR FIRST DEGREE.

W. M. Why were you neither barefoot nor shod?

S. W. This was according to an ancient Israelitish custom. We read in the book of Ruth, that this was the manner in former times concerning redeeming and concerning changing for to confirm all things; a man plucked off his shoe and gave it to his neighbor, and this was a testimony in Israel. This, therefore, was done to show the sincerity of our intentions in the business we were then engaged upon.

W. M. Why were you hoodwinked and a cable-tow about your neck?

S. W. For three reasons: first, that as I was then in darkness, so should I keep the world without in the future, as relates to the secrets of Masonry, until they should obtain them as lawfully as I was then about to do; second, that my heart should be taught to conceal before my eyes beheld the beauties of Masonry; third, should I have refused to submit to the forms and ceremonies of Masonry, being found unworthy to be taken by the hand as a brother, I might, by the help of the cable-tow, be conducted out of the Lodge without being allowed to discover even the form thereof.

W. M. Why were you caused to give three distinct knocks?

S. W. For two reason: first, to alarm the Lodge and inform the Worshipful Master that I was prepared for initiation; second, to remind me of a certain text in Scripture, "Ask and ye shall receive; seek and ye shall find; knock and it shall be opened unto you."

ENTERED APPRENTICE, OR FIRST DEGREE.

W. H. How did you apply that text to your then situation?

S. W. I asked the recommendation of a friend to be made a Mason; through his recommendation I sought initiation; I knocked at the door of the Lodge and it was opened unto me.

W. M. Why were you received on the point of a sharp instrument?

S. W. It was to signify that as that was an instrument of torture to the flesh, so should the remembrance thereof be to my conscience, should I ever presume to reveal any of the secrets of Masonry unlawfully.

W. M. Why were you caused to kneel and attend prayer?

S. W. Because no man should ever enter upon any great and important undertaking without first invoking the blessing of Deity.

W. M. Why were you asked in whom you put your trust?

S. W. Because, agreeable to an ancient Masonic custom, no Atheist could be made a Mason; it was, therefore, necessary that I should profess my belief in Deity, otherwise no oath would be binding upon me.

W. M. Why were you taken by the right hand, ordered to arise, follow your guide and fear no danger?

S. W. It was to show that although at that time I could neither foresee nor prevent danger, I was in the hands of a trusty friend, in whose fidelity I might with safety confide.

ENTERED APPRENTICE, OR FIRST DEGREE.

W. M. Why were conducted once about the altar?

S. W. That the brethren might see I was duly and truly prepared.

W. M. Why were you caused to meet with these several obstructions on your passage?

S. W. Because in every regular and well-governed Lodge there is a representation of King Solomon's Temple, in which we learn there were guards stationed at the South, West and East gates, to see that none passed or repassed but such as were duly qualified and had their permission. It was therefore necessary that I should meet with these several obstruction, in order that I might be duly examined before I could be made a Mason.

W. M. Why were you caused to kneel on your naked left knee?

S. W. Because the left was supposed to be the weaker part of man; it was, therefore, to show that it was the weaker part of Masonry I was then entering upon, it being that of an Entered Apprentice.

W. M. Why were you caused to lay your right hand on the Holy Bible, square and compasses?

S. W. Because the right hand was supposed by our ancient brethren to be the seat of fidelity, which was said sometimes to be represented by two right hands joined, at other by two human figures holding each other by the right hand. The right hand, therefore, was made use of as a token of our sincerity, and a pledge of our fidelity in the business we were then engaged upon.

W. M. Why were you presented with the lambskin apron, which is the true badge of a Mason?

ENTERED APPRENTICE, OR FIRST DEGREE.

S. W. Because the lamb has in all ages been deemed an emblem of innocence; he, therefore, who wears the lamb-skin as a badge of Masonry, is thereby continually reminded of that purity of life and conduct which is essentially necessary to his gaining admission into that celestial Lodge above, where the Supreme Architect of the Universe presides.

W. M. Why were you requested to deposit something of a metallic kind?

S. W. It was to remind me of my then extremely poor and penniless situation; should I ever afterwards meet a friend, more especially a brother, in like circumstances, that I should contribute as liberally to his relief as I could do without inconvenience to myself.

W. M. Why were you placed in the North-east corner, as the youngest Entered Apprentice?

S. W. Because in operative masonry the first stone of a building is usually placed in the North-east corner; I was, therefore, placed there to receive those first instructions upon which to build my future moral and Masonic edifice.

SECTION THIRD.

W. M. What is a Lodge?

S. W. A certain number of Masons, duly assembled, with the Holy Bible, square and compasses, and charter, or warrant, empowering them to work.

W. M. Where did our ancient brethren usually meet?

S. W. On a high hill or in a low dale.

W. M. Why so?

ENTERED APPRENTICE, OR FIRST DEGREE.

S. W. The better to detect the approach of cowans and eavesdroppers, either ascending or descending.

W. M. What is the form of a Lodge?

S. W. An oblong.

W. M. How long?

S. W. From East to West.

W. M. How broad?

S. W. From North to South.

W. M. How high?

S. W. From the earth to the heavens.

W. M. How deep?

S. W. From its surface to its centre.

W. M. Why is it of such vast dimensions?

S. W. To show the universality of Masonry, and that Masonic charity should be equally extensive.

W. M. What supports this grand fabric?

S. W. Three great pillars.

W. M. What are they called?

S. W. Wisdom, Strength and Beauty.

W. M. Why are they called?

S. W. Because it is necessary there should be Wisdom to contrive, Strength to support, and Beauty to adorn all great important undertakings.

W. M. By whom are they represented?

S. W. By the Worshipful Master, Senior and Junior Wardens.

W. M. How do they represent them?

S. W. The Worshipful Master represents the pillar of Wisdom, it being supposed that he has wisdom to open his Lodge, set the craft to work and give them proper instructions. The Senior Warden represents the pillar of Strength, it being his duty

ENTERED APPRENTICE, OR FIRST DEGREE.

to assist the Worshipful Master in opening and closing his Lodge; to pay the craft their wages, if any be due, and see that none go away dissatisfied, harmony being the strength and support of all societies, more especailly our own. The Junior Warden represents the pillar of Beauty, it being his duty to observe the sun at its meridian height, which is the glory and beauty of the day.

W. M. What covering has a Lodge?

S. W. A clouded canopy or star-decked heavens, where all good Masons hope at last to arrive, by the aid of that theological ladder which Jacob in his wisdom saw ascending from earth to heaven, the three principal rounds of which are denominated Faith, Hope and Charity; and which admonish us to have faith in God, hope in immortality, and charity to all mankind.

W. M. Which of these is the principal?

S. W. The third, Charity.

W. M. Why so?

S. W. Because our faith may be lost in sight, hope ends in fruition, but charity extends beyond the grave, through the boundless realms of eternity.

W. M. What furniture has a Lodge?

S. W. The Holy Bible, square and compasses.

W. M. To whom are they dedicated?

S. W. The Bible points out the path that leads to happiness, and is dedicated to God; the square teaches us to regulate our conduct by the principles of morality and virtue, and is dedicated to the Master; the compasses teaches us to limit our desires in every station, and is dedicated to the craft.

ENTERED APPRENTICE, OR FIRST DEGREE.

W. M. Why are they thus disposed of?

S. W. The Bible is dedicated to the service of God, because it is the inestimable gift of God to man, and on it we obligate a newly admitted brother; the square to the Master, because, being the proper emblem of his office, it is constantly to remind him of the duty he owes to the Lodge over which he is appointed to preside; and the compasses to the craft, because, by a due attention to its use, they are taught to regulate their desire and keep their passions within due bounds.

W. M. What are the ornaments of a Lodge?

S. W. The Mosaic Pavement, the Indented Tessel and the Blazing Star.

W. M. What are they?

S. W. The Mosaic Pavement is a representation of the grand floor of King Solomon's Temple; the Indented Tessel, that beautiful tessellated border or skirting which surrounded it; and the Blazing Star, in the centre, is commemorative of the star which appeared to guide the wise men of the East to the place of our Saviour's nativity.

W. M. Of what are they emblematical?

S. W. The Mosaic Pavement is emblematical of human life, chequered with good and evil. The beautiful border which surrounds it, those blessings and comforts which reliance on Divine Providence, which is hieroglyphically represented by the Blazing Star in the centre.

W. M. How man lights has a Lodge?

S. W. Three..

ENTERED APPRENTICE, OR FIRST DEGREE.

W. M. How are they situated?
S. W. East, West and South.
W. M. None in the North?
S. W. None.
W. M. Why not?
S. W. Because of the situation of King Solomon's Temple, it being situated so far North of the ecliptic that the sun and moon at their meridian height could dart no rays in the northern part of it; and so we Masonically term the North a place of darkness.
W. M. How many jewels has a Lodge?
S. W. Six: three movable and three immovable.
W. M. What are the immovable jewels?
S. W. The Square, Level and Plumb.
W. M. What do they Masonically teach us?
S. W. The Square teaches morality, the Level equality, and the Plumb rectitude of life.
W. M. What are the movable jewels?
S. W. The Rough Ashler, the Perfect Ashler and the Trestle-Board.
W. M. What are they?
S. W. The Rough Ashler is a stone taken from the quarry in its rude and natural state. The Perfect Ashler is a stone made ready by the hands of the workmen to be adjusted by the tools of the Fellow Craft. The Trestle-Board is for the Master workman to draw his designs upon.
W. M. Of what do they remind us?
S. W. By the Rough Ashler we are reminded of our rude and imperfect state by nature; by the Perfect Ashler, that state of perfection at which we hope to arrive by a virtuous education, our own en-

ENTERED APPRENTICE, OR FIRST DEGREE.

deavors and the blessing of God; and by the Trestle-Board we are reminded that as the operative workman erects his temporal building agreeably to the rules and designs laid down by the Master on his Trestle-Board, so should we, both operative and speculative, endeavor to erect our spiritual building agreeably to the rules and designs laid down by the Supreme Architect of the Universe in the Book of Life, which is our spiritual Trestle-Board.

W. M. How should a Lodge be situated?

S. W. Due East and West.

W. M. Why so?

S. W. Because that was the situation of King Solomon's Temple.

W. M. Why was King Solomon's Temple so situated?

S. W. Because, after Moses had safely conducted the children of Israel through the Red Sea, when pursued by Pharaoh and his hosts, he then, by divine command, erected a tabernacle and set it due East and West, in order to perpetuate the remembrance of the mighty East wind by which their miraculous deliverance was wrought, and also to receive the rays of the rising Sun; and as the tabernacle was an exact model of King Solomon's Temple, therefore all Lodges should be situated due East and West.

W. M. To whom were Lodges anciently dedicated?

S. W. To King Solomon.

W M. Why so?

S. W. Because he was our first Most Excellent Grand Master.

ENTERED APPRENTICE, OR FIRST DEGREE.

W. M. To whom are they dedicated in modern times?

S. W. To St. John the Baptist and St. John the Evangelist, who were eminent patrons of Masonry; and since their time there is represented in every regular and well-governed Lodge a certaiin Point within a Circle; the Point representing an individual brother, the Circle representing the boundary line of his duty to God and man, beyond which he is never to suffer his passions, prejudices or interests to betray him on any occasion. This Circle is embordered by two perpendicular parallel lines representing St. John the Baptist and St. John the Evangelist, who were perfect parallels in Christianity as well as Masonry; and upon the vertex rests the book of Holy Scriptures, which point out the whole duty of man. In going round this Circle we necessarily touch upon these two lines, as well as upon the Holy Scriptures; and while a Mason keeps himself thus circumscribed, it is impossible that he should materially err.

W. M. What are the tenets of your profession?

S. W. Brotherly Love, Relief and Truth.

By the exercise of brotherly love we are taught to regard the whole human species as one family, the high and low, the rich and poor; who, as created by one Almighty Parent, and inhabitants of the same planet, are to aid, support and protect each other. On this principle, Masonry unites men of every country, sect and opinion, and conciliates true friendship among those who might otherwise have remained at a perpetual distance.

ENTERED APPRENTICE, OR FIRST DEGREE.

To relieve the distressed is a duty incumbent on all men, but particularly on Masons, who are linked together by an indissoluble chain of sincere affection. To soothe the unhappy, to sympathize with their misfortunes, to compassionate their miserieis and to restore peace to their troubled minds, is the grand aim we have in view. On this basis we form our friendships and establish our connections.

Truth is a divine attribute and the foundation of every virtue. To be good and true is the first lesson we are taught in Masonry. On this theme we contemplate, and by its dictates endeavor to regulate our conduct. Hence, while influenced by this principle, hypocrisy and deceit are unknown among us, sincerity and plain dealing distinguish us, and the heart and tongue join in promoting each other's welfare and rejoicing in each other's prosperity.

W. M. Brother, you informed me that I should know you by certain signs, a token, a word, and the perfect points of your entrance. You have given me the signs, token and word. I now require you to explain to me the perfect points of your entrance. How many and what are they?

S. W. They are four, the Guttural, the Pectoral, the Manual and the Pedestal; which allude to the four cardinal virtues, Temperance, Fortitude, Prudence and Justice.

Temperance is that due restraint upon our affections and passions which renders the body tame and governable, and frees the mind from the allurements of vice. This virtue should be the constant practice

ENTERED APPRENTICE, OR FIRST DEGREE.

of every Mason, as he is thereby taught to avoid excess, or contracting any licentious or vicious habit, the indulgence of which might lead him to disclose some of those valuable secrets which he has promised to conceal and never reveal, and which would consequently subject him to the contempt and detestation of all good Masons, as well as to the penalty of his obligation, which alludes to the Guttural.

Fortitude is that noble and steady purpose of the mind whereby we are enabled to undergo any pain, peril or danger, when prudentially deemed expedient. This virtue is equally distant from rashness and cowardice; and, like the former, should be deeply impressed upon the mind of every Mason, as a safeguard or security against any illegal attack that may be made, by force or otherwise, to extort from him any of those secrets with which he has been so solemnly intrusted; and which was emblematically represented upon his first admission into the Lodge, where he was received on the point of a sharp instrument at his naked left breast, which alludes to the Pectoral.

Prudence teaches us to regulate our lives and actions agreebly to the dictates of our reason, and is that habit by which we wisely judge and prudentially determine on all things relative to our present as well as to our future happiness. This virtue should be the peculiar characteristic of every Mason, not only for the government of his conduct while in the Lodge, but also when abroad in the world. It should be particularly attended to in all strange and mixed companies, never to let fall the least sign

ENTERED APPRENTICE, OR FIRST DEGREE.

token or word whereby the secrets of Masonry might be unlawfully obtained; especially bearing in mind that memorable period when on his left knee bare bent, his right forming a square, his left hand supporting the Holy Bible, square and compasses, his right resting thereon, which alludes to the Manual.

Justice is that standard or boundary of right which enables us to render to every man his just due without distinction. This virtue is not only consistent with Divine and human laws, but is the very cement and support of civil society; and as justice in a great measure constitutes the real good man, so should it be the invariable practice of every Mason never to deviate from the minutest principles thereof, ever remembering the time when he was placed in the North-east corner of the Lodge, his feet forming a right angle, which alludes to the Pedestal.

W. M. How did Entered Apprentices serve their Master in former times, and how should they in modern?

S. W. With freedom, fervency and zeal.

W. M. How are they represented?

S. W. By Chalk, Charcoal and Clay.

W. M. Why do they represent them?

S. W. Because there is nothing freer than Chalk, which, upon the slightest touch, leaves a trace behind; nothing more fervent than Charcoal, to which, when properly lighted, the most obdurate metal will yield; nothing more zealous than Clay, or mother earth, which is constantly employed for man's use, and is an emblem to remind him that as from it we came, so to it we must all return.

ENTERED APPRENTICE, OR FIRST DEGREE.

W. M. This, my brethren, ends the lecture in this degree.

CEREMONY OF CLOSING AN ENTERED APPRENTICES' LODGE.

At the conclusion of the lecture, the following method is adopted for closing a Lodge of Entered Apprentices:

W. M. to J. D. Brother Junior Deacon, what is the last great care of Masons when in Lodge assembled?

J. D. To see that the Lodge is duly tyled, Worshiful Master.

W. M. to J. D. Perform that duty; inform the Tyler that I am about to close this Lodge of Entered Apprentices.

The Junior Deacon obeys the order.

J. D. The Lodge is duly tyled, Worshipful Master.

W. M. to J. D. How are we tyled, brother Junior Deacon?

J. D. By a brother Master Mason without the door, armed with the proper instrument of his office.

W. M. What are his duties there?

J. D. To keep off all cowans and eavesdroppers, and to see that none pass or repass but such as are duly qualified and have permission from the Worshipful Master.

The Master seats the Deacon by one rap.

W. M. to S. W. Brother Senior Warden, as an Entered Apprentice, from whence came you?

S. W. From the Lodge of the Holy Saints John at Jerusalem.

ENTERED APPRENTICE, OR FIRST DEGREE.

W. M. What came you here to do?

S. W. To learn to subdue my passions and improve myself in Masonry.

W. M. Then I presume you are a Mason?

S. W. I am so taken and accepted among brothers and fellows.

W. M. Where were you made an Entered Apprentice?

S. W. In a just and lawfully constituted Lodge of Entered Apprentices.

W. M. How many anciently composed a Lodge of Entered Apprentices?

S. W. Seven or more.

W. M. When composed of only seven, who were they?

S. W. The Worshipful Master, Senior Warden, Junior Warden, Treasurer, Secretary, Senior Deacon and Junior Deacon.

W. M. What is the Junior Deacon's place in the Lodge?

S. W. On the right of the Senior Warden in the West.

W. M. What are your duties there, brother Junior Deacon?

J. D. To carry messages from the Senior Warden in the West to the Junior Warden in the South, and elsewhere about the Lodge, as he may direct; and to see that the Lodge is duly tyled.

W. M. What is the Senior Deacon's place in the Lodge?

J. D. On the right of the Worshipful Master in the East.

ENTERED APPRENTICE, OR FIRST DEGREE.

W. M. What are your duties there, brother Senior Deacon?

S. D. To carry orders from the Worshipful Master in the East to the Senior Warden in the West, and elsewhere about the Lodge, as he may direct; to welcome and accommodate visiting brethren; to receive and conduct candidates.

W. M. What is the Secretary's place in the Lodge?

S. D. On the left of the Worshipful Master in the East.

The Master now calls up the Secretary, Treasurer, Junior and Senior Wardens by two raps.

W. M. What are your duties there, brother Seretary?

Sec. To observe the Worshipful Master's will and pleasure; to record the proceedings of the Lodge; to receive all moneys, and to pay them into the hands of the Treasurer.

W. M. What is the Treasurer's place in the Lodge?

Sec. On the right of the Worshipful Master in East.

W. M. What are your duties there, brother Treasurer?

Treas. To receive all moneys from the hand of the Secretary; keep just and regular account of the same, and pay them out at the Worshipful Master's will and pleasure, with the consent of the Lodge.

W. M. What is the Junior Warden's station in the Lodge?

Treas. In the South.

ENTERED APPRENTICE, OR FIRST DEGREE.

W. M. Why are you in the South, brother Junior Warden? What are your duties there?

J. W. As the Sun in the South at its meridian height is the glory and beauty of the day, so stands the Junior Warden in the South, the better to observe the time; to call the craft from labor to refreshment; to superintend them during the hours thereof, and see that they do not convert the purposes of refreshment into intemperance and excess; to call them on again in due season, that the Worshipful Master may have pleasure and the craft profit thereby.

W. M. What is the Senior Warden's station in the Lodge?

J. W. In the West.

W. M. Why are you in the West, brother Senior Warden? What are your duties there?

S. W. As the Sun is in the West at the close of the day, so is the Senior Warden in the West, to assist the Worshipful Master in opening and closing his Lodge; to pay the craft their wages, if any be due, and see that none go away dissatisfied, harmony being the strength and support of all societies, more especially of ours.

W. M. What is the Worshipful Master's station in the Lodge?

S. W. In the East.

W. M. Why is he in the East, brother Senior Warden? What are his duties there?

S. W. As the Sun rises in the East to open and govern the day, so rises the Worshipful Master in the East to open and govern his Lodge; to set the

ENTERED APPRENTICE, OR FIRST DEGREE.

craft to work, and give them good and wholesome instruction for their labors.

The Worshipful Master now calls up the Lodge with three raps, himself rising last.

W. M. to S. W. Brother Senior Warden, it is my will and pleasure that this Lodge of Entered Apprentices be now closed. Communicate this order to the Junior Warden in the South, and he to the craft for their government.

S. W. to J. W. Brother Junior Warden, it is the will and pleasure of the Worshipful Master in the East that this Lodge of Entered Apprentices be now closed. Communicate this order to the craft for their government.

J. W. to Lodge. Brethren, it is the will and pleasure of the Worshipful Master in the East, communicated to me by the Senior Warden in the West, that this Lodge of Entered Apprentices be now closed; take notice and govern yourselves accordingly.— Look to the East!

The signs are now given and the raps passed once about the stations.

W. M. to Lodge. In the name of God and of the Holy Saints John, I declare this Lodge of Entered Apprentices closed in form. Brother Junior Deacon, inform the Tyler.

The Master now reuests all those present who are not Master Masons to retire. The Deacons perform the duties assigned to them and are then seated by one rap.

W. M. to S. W. Brother Senior Warden, proceed to satisfy yourself that all present are Master Masons.

ENTERED APPRENTICE, OR FIRST DEGREE.

When this order is obeyed, the Senior Warden reports to the Master:

S. W. to W. M. All present are Master Masons.

The Master calls up the Senior and Junior Deacons by one rap.

W. M. to J. D. Brother Junior Deacon, what is the first great care of Masons when in Lodge assembled?

J. D. to W. M. To see that the Lodge is duly tyled, Worship Master.

W. M. Perform that duty, and inform the Tyler that we are about to resume labor as Master Masons.

The Junior Deacon obeys this order, and reports to the Worshipful Master as follows:

J. D. The Lodge is duly tyled, Worshipful Master.

W. M. How are we tyled, brother Junior Deacon?

J. D. By a brother Master Mason without the door, armed with the proper instrument of his office.

W. M. What are his duties there?

J. D. To keep off all cowans and eavesdroppers, and to see that none pass or repass but such as are duly ualified and have permission from the Worshipful Master.

The Master gives one rap, which seats the Deacons.

W. M. to J. W. Brother Junior Warden, how goes the hour?

J. W. to W. M. One hour past high twelve, Worshipful Master.

W. M. It being one hour past high twelve, you will call the craft from refreshment to labor on the third degree.

ENTERED APPRENTICE, OR FIRST DEGREE.

The Junior Warden calls up the Lodge by three raps.

J. W. to Lodge. Brethren, it is the will and pleasure of the Worshipful Master in the East that this Lodge be called from refreshment to labor on the third degree; take notice and govern yourselves accordingly.—Look to the East!

The signs are given and the raps passed about the stations three times, as at opening. The Master then continues:

W. M. to Lodge. I declare this Lodge at labor on the third degree. Brother Junior Deacon, inform the Tyler. Brother Senior Deacon, arrange the three Great Lights.

The Junior Deacon reports, and the Great Lights are displayed to correspond with the degree.

W. M. to S. W. Brother Senior Warden, have you anything in the West to come before this Lodge of Master Masons?

S. W. Nothing in the West, Worshipful Master.

W. M. to J. W. Anything in the South, brother Junior Warden?

J. W. Nothing in the South, Worshipful Master.

W. M. to Sec. Brother Secretary, have you anything on your table?

Sec. Nothing, Worshipful Master.

W. M. to J. D. Brother Junior Deacon, what is the last great care of Masons when in Lodge assembled?

J. D. To see that the Lodge is duly tyled, Worshipful Master.

W. M. Perform that duty, and inform the Tyler

ENTERED APPRENTICE, OR FIRST DEGREE.

that I am about to close this Lodge of Master Masons.

The Junior Deacon opens the door and communicates the Master's order, and reports:

J. D. to W. M. The Lodge is duly tyled, Worshipful Master.

W. M. How are we tyled, brother Junior Deacon?

J. D. By a brother Master Mason with out the door, armed with the proper instrument of his office.

W. M. What are his duties there?

J. D. To keep off all cowans and eavesdroppers, and to see that none pass or repass but such as are duly qualified and have permission from the Worshipful Master.

The Worshipful Master now seats the Deacons by one rap.

W. M. to S. W. Are you a Master Mason?

S. W. I am.

W. M. What induced you to become a Master Mason?

S. W. In order that I might receive Masters' wages, and better to be enabled to support myself and family, and contribute to the relief of poor distressed Master Masons, their widows and orphans.

W. M. Where were you made a Master Mason?

S. W. In a just and lawfully constituted Lodge of Master Masons.

W. M. How many anciently composed a Lodge of Master Masons?

S. W. Three or more.

W. M. When composed of only three, who were they?

ENTERED APPRENTICE, OR FIRST DEGREE.

S. W. The Worshipful Master, Senior Warden and Junior Warden.

W. M. What is the Junior Warden's station in the Lodge?

S. W. In the South.

W. M. to J. W. Why are you in the South, brother Junior Warden? What are your duties there?

J. W. to W. M. As the Sun in the South at its meridian height is the glory and beauty of the day, so stands the Junior Warden in the South, the better to observe the time; to call the craft from labor to refreshment; to superintend them during the hours thereof, and see that they do not convert the purposes of refreshment into intemperance and excess; to call them on again in due season, that the Worshipful Master may have pleasure and the craft profit thereby.

W. M. to J. W. What is the Senior Warden's station in the Lodge?

J. W. In the West.

W. M. to S. W. Why are you in the West, brother Senior Warden? What are your duties there?

S. W. to W. M. As the Sun is in the West at the close of the day, so is the Senior Warden in the West to assist the Worshipful Master in opening and closing his Lodge; to pay the craft their wages, if any be due, and see that none go away dissatisfied, harmony being the strength and support of all societies, more especially of ours.

W. M. to S. W. What is the Worshipful Master's station in the Lodge?

S. W. to W. M. In the East.

ENTERED APPRENTICE, OR FIRST DEGREE.

W. M. to S. W. Why is he in the East, brother Senior Warden? What are his duties there?

S. W. to W. M. As the Sun rises in the East to open and govern the day, so rises the Worshipful Master in the East to open and govern his Lodge; to set the craft to work, and give them good and wholesome instruction for their labors.

The Master calls up the Lodge by three raps.

W. M. to S. W. Brother Senior Warden, it is my will and pleasure that ——— Lodge number ——— be now closed. Communicate this order to the Junior Warden in the South, and he to the craft for their government.

S. W. to J. W. Brother Junior Warden, it is the will and pleasure of the Worshipful Master in the East that ——— Lodge number ——— be now closed; communicate this order to the craft of their government.

J. W. to Lodge. Brethren, it is the will and pleasure of the Worshipful Master in the East, communicated to me by the Senior Warden in the West, that ——— Lodge number ——— be now closed; take notice and govern yourselves accordingly.—Look to the East!

The signs are now given, the raps passed about the stations three times, and the usual prayer is offered. When this is done, the Master asks the following questions:

W. M. to S. W. Brother Senior Warden, how do Masons meet?

S. W. Upon the level, Worshipful Master.

W. M. Brother Junior Warden, how do Masons act?

ENTERED APPRENTICE, OR FIRST DEGREE.

J. W. Upon the plumb, Worshipful Master.

W. M. to Lodge. And they part upon the square. So may we meet, act and part. May the blessings of heaven rest upon us and all regular Masons! May brotherly love prevail, and every moral and social virtue cement us! In the name of God and the Holy Saints John I declare this Lodge closed in form. Brother Junior Deason, inform the Tyler..

The Master gives three raps and the craft are dismissed. The Junior Deason gives three raps at the door, which are answered by the Tyler, and as soon as the Master's orders are communicated to him, the door is thrown open for the brethren to depart.

Meanwhile the Senior Deacon closes the Great Lights, and places them on the Secretary's table, who secures them in the proper place. The Lesser Lights are removed, and the Wardens reverse their columns, down in the West, erect in the South.

A SHORT METHOD OF CLOSING A LODGE OF ENTERED APPRENTICES.

The foregoing is the *proper* method of calling a Lodge up and down, but when time is an object, the following method is sometimes adopted:

W. M. to J. D. Brother Junior Deacon, what is the last great care of Masons when in Lodge assembled?

J. D. To see that the Lodge is duly tyled, Worshipful Master.

W. M. Perform that duty, and inform the Tyler that I am about to close this Lodge of Entered Apprentices. The Deacon obeys the order.

ENTERED APPRENTICE, OR FIRST DEGREE.

J. D. to W. M. The Lodge is duly tyled, Worshipful Master.

The Master calls up the Lodge.

W. M. to Lodge. Brethren, I declare this Lodge of Entered Apprentices closed, and labor resumed on the third degree, waiving all further ceremonies, Brother Junior Deacon, inform the Tyler. Brother Senio Warden, attend to the three Great Lights.

The Lodge is now purged, tyled and closed in the third degree. *(See pages 67 to 71.)*

CALLING OFF AND ON.

The routine of calling off the craft from labor to refreshment, and on again from refreshment to labor, is the same in all of the three degrees. The Master asks the following uestions:

W. M. to J. W. Brother Junior Warden, how goes the hour?

J. W. High twelve, Worshipful Master.

W. M. to J. W. It being high twelve, you will call the craft from labor to refreshment for the space of fifteen minutes. *(More or less, as the case may be.)*

The Junior Warden calls up the Lodge by three raps.

J. W. to Lodge. Brethren, it is the will and pleasure of the Worshapful Master in the East that this Lodge now be called from labor to refreshment for the space of fifteen minutes.—Look to the East!

The craft all turn to the Master in the East.

W. M. to Lodge. I declare this Lodge at refreshment for the space of fifteen minutes. Brother Junior Deacon, inform the Tyler.

ENTERED APPRENTICE, OR FIRST DEGREE.

The Master dismisses the craft by one rap; the Junior Warden communicates the Master's order to the Tyler, who opens the door.

The Great Lights are closed, the Senior and Junior Wardens reverse their columns, down in the West, erect in the South; and the craft disperse in charge of the Junior Warden, who reassembles them in the Lodge at the expiration of the time appointed for refreshment. The Lodge is then tyled in the same manner as in the opening, and the Master proceeds as follows:

W. M. to J. W. Brother Junior Warden, how goes the hour?

J. W. One hour past high twelve, Worshipful Master.

W. M. to J. W. It being one hour past high twelve, you will call the craft from refreshment to labor on the ——— degree.

The Junior Warden calls up the Lodge by three raps.

J. W. to Lodge. Brethren, it is the will and pleasure of the Worshipful Master in the East that this Lodge be now called from refreshment to labor on the ——— degree; take notice and govern yourselves accordingly.—Look to the East!

The signs are given and the raps are passed about the stations according to the degree the Lodge is called to labor on, with the same care as at opening. Then the Master says:

W. M. to Lodge. I declare the Lodge at labor on the ——— degree; brother Junior Deacon, inform the Tyler.

ENTERED APPRENTICE, OR FIRST DEGREE.

The Junior Deacon goes to the door and gives three knocks upon it, which are answered with the same number of knocks by the Tyler, who opens the door; the Junior Deacon informs him on what degree the Lodge is at work, and he then closes the door and the Tyler locks it. The Junior Deacon then reports as follows:

J. D. to W. M. The Lodge is duly tyled, Worshipful Master.

W. M. to J. D. How are we tyled, Brother Junior Deacon?

J. D. By a brother Master Mason without the door, armed with the proper instrument of his office.

W. M. What are his duties there?

J. D. To keep off all cowans and eavesdroppers, and to see that none pass or repass but such as are duly qualified and have permission from the Worshipful Master.

The Master seats the Junior Deacon by one rap. The Senior and Junior Wardens reverse their columns, erect in the West, down in the South, and the Great Lights are arranged in the manner suitable to the degree in which the Lodge is called to labor.

FELLOW CRAFT, OR SECOND DEGREE.

As stated in the Entered Apprentice degree, the ceremonies of initiation, passing and raising are performed after the transaction of the regular business, which latter can only be done in a Master Masons' Lodge. The Lodge is therefore opened in the third degree, and the regular business of the Lodge is first attended to; after which the Lodge is called off in the third degree, and remains so until opened in the second degree for the purpose of passing a candidate.

OPENING A LODGE OF MASTER MASONS.

The ceremony of opening a Lodge in the third degree is conducted as follows: When the regular time for opening has arrived, the Master repairs to his station and calls the Lodge to order with one rap of his gavel. The door is shut, the brethren clothe themselves and take their seats; the officers put on their jewels; the Wardens dispose of their columns, down in the West, erect in the South; the Deacons take their rods; the Secretary lays his books and papers and the three Great Lights upon his table, and in a few moments the Lodge is silent and in order for the opening. The Master then proceeds as follows:

W. M. to S. W. Brother Senior Warden, proceed to satisfy yourself that all present are Master Masons.

FELLOW CRAFT, OR SECOND DEGREE.

The Senior Warden rises and makes a personal observation of every one that is present. He then requests the Senior and Junior Deacons to give to him, in a whisper, the pass of a Master Mason, and to demand it, under the same conditions, from each person present except the Worshipful Master, Senior Warden and Junior Warden. After this is done, the Junior Deacon communicates the pass to the Senior Deacon and he to the Worshipful Master.

W. M. to S. W. The pass is ———.

S. W. to W. M. All present are Master Masons, Worshipful Master.

When any one addresses the Master during any Masonic ceremony, he must rise and salute.

The Worshipful Master calls up the Senior Deacon and Junior Deacon by one rap.

W. M. to J. D. Brother Junior Deaonc, what is the first great care of Masons when in Lodge assembled?

J. D. to W. M. To see that the Lodge is duly tyled, Worshipful Master.

W. M. to J. D. Perform that duty. Inform the Tyler that I am about to open a Lodge of Master Masons, and direct him to tyle accordingly.

The Junior Deacon opens the door without knocking, and satisfies himself that the Tyler is at his post, he then communicates to him the Master's orders and shuts the door. The Tyler then locks the door on the outside.

J. D. to W. M. The Lodge is duly tyled, Worshipful Master.

W. M. to J. D. How are we tyled, brother Junior Deacon?

FELLOW CRAFT, OR SECOND DEGREE.

J. D. to W. M. By a brother Master Mason without the door, armed with the proper instrument of his office.

W. M. to J. D. What are his duties there?

J. D. to W. M. To keep off all cowans and eavesdroppers, and to see that none pass or repass but such as are duly qualified and have permission from the Worshipful Master.

The Master then seats the Senior and Junior Deacons with one rap.

W. M. to S. W. Are you a Master Mason?

S. W. I am.

W. M. What induced you to become a Master Mason?

S. W. In order that I might receive Masters' wages, and be thereby better enabled to support myself and family, and contribute to the relief of poor, distressed Master Masons, their widows and orphans.

W. M. to S. W. Where were you made a Master Mason?

S. W. to M. W. In a just and lawfully constituted Lodge of Master Masons.

After having rehearsed as much of the lecture as he deems necessary, the Master proceeds as follows:

W. M. to S. W. How many anciently composed a Lodge of Master Masons?

S. W. to W. M. Three or more.

W. M. to S. W. When composed of only three, who were they?

S. W. to W. M. The Worshipful Master, Senior Warden and Junior arden.

W. M. to S. W. What is the Junior arden's station in the Lodge?

FELLOW CRAFT, OR SECOND DEGREE.

S. W. to W. M. In the South.

W. M. Why are you in the South, brother Junior Warden? What are your duties?

J. W. As the Sun in the South at its meridian height is the glory and beauty of the day, so stands the Junior Warden in the South, the better to observe the time; to call the craft from labor to refreshment; to superintend them during the hours thereof, and see that they do not convert the purposes of refreshment into intemperance and excess; to call them in again in due season, that the Worshipful Master may have pleasure and the craft profit thereby.

W. M. What is the Senior Warden's station in the Lodge?

J. W. In the West.

W. M. Why are you in the West, brother Senior Warden? What are your duties there?

S. . As the Sun is in the West at the close of the day, so is the Senior Warden in the West to assist the Worshipful Master in opening and closing his Lodge; to pay the craft their wages, if any be due, and see that none go away dissatisfied, harmony being the strength and support of all societies, more especially of ours.

W. M. What is the Worshipful Master's station in the Lodge?

S. W. In the East.

W. M. Why is he in the East, brother Senior Warden? What are his duties there?

S. W. As the Sun rises in the East to open and govern the day, so rises the Worshipful Master in

FELLOW CRAFT, OR SECOND DEGREE.

the East to open and govern his Lodge; to set the craft to work, and give them good and wholesome instruction for their labors.

This closes the opening lecture. The Master gives three raps, which call up the Lodge, he rising last.

W. M. Brother Senior Warden, it is my will and pleasure that ——— Lodge number ——— be now opened on the third degree of Masonry, for the dispatch of such business as may regularly come before it, under the usual Masonic restrictions. Communicate this order to the Junior Warden in the South and he to the craft for their government.

S. W. to J. W. *(turning to that officer in the South.)* Brother Junior Warden, it is the will and pleasure of the Worshipful Master in the East that ——— Lodge number ——— be now opened on the third degree of Masonry, for the dispatch of such business as may regularly come before it, under the usual Masonic restrictions. Communicate this order to the craft for their government.

J. W. to Lodge. Brethren, it is the will and pleasure of the Worshipful Master in the East, communicated to me by the Senior Warden in the West, that ——— Lodge number ——— be now opened on the third degree of Masonry, for the dispatch of such business as may regularly come before it, under the usual Masonic restrictions. Take notice and govern yourselves accordingly.—Look to the East!

W. M. to Lodge. Brethren, together, and the signs.

The craft all face towards the Worshipful Master, who makes, slowly and distinctly, the signs of an

FELLOW CRAFT, OR SECOND DEGREE.

Entered Apprentice, Fellow Craft and Master Mason, successively, which are imitated simultaneously by the craft.

After the signs have been made the Junior Warden gives on rap with his gavel, followed by the Senior Warden in the West and by the Master in the East. These raps are passed thrice about the stations.

The Master now takes off his hat and says: "Let us pray."

The prayer is offered by the Master or Chaplain. After prayer the Master announces to the Lodge:

W. M. In the name of God and the Holy Saints John, I declare ——— Lodge number ——— opened in form on the third degree. Brother Junior Deacon, inform the Tyler.

The Master seats the craft by one rap. The Junior Deacon goes to the door and knocks thrice upon it, on which it is opened by the Tyler, to whom the Junior Deacon announces that the Lodge is opened in the third degree. He then shuts the door, which is locked on the outside by the Tyler.

J. D. to W. M. The duty is performed, Worshipful Master.

The Master seats the Junior Deacon by one rap. While this is in progress, the Senior Deacon takes the three Great Lights from the Secretary's table and arranges them duly upon the altar, the Bible laying open at Ecclesiastics xii, and both points of the compasses above the suare.

The Lesser Lights are placed in their proper position, two at the North-east and North-west corners

FELLOW CRAFT, OR SECOND DEGREE.

of the altar, and the third between them, a little further Northward. The Wardens reverse their columns, erect in the West, down in the South.

As has already been stated, all matters of business are transacter in the Lodge when opened on the third degree; when the work of initiation is to be done, the Lodge must be called off in the third degree, and remain so until duly opened in the first degree; when an Entered Appretice is to be passed, the Lodge is called off in the third degree, and remains so while the second degree is opened; if a Fellow Craft is to be raised the Lodge remains in the Master Masons' degree.

After the ceremonies of opening are concluded, the Master requests the Secretary to read the minutes of their last regular communication. This being done, the Master asks as follows:

W. M. to S. W. Brother Senior Warden, have you any alterations to propose?

If the Senior Warden has any remarks to make, he now does so, first making the sign of a Master Mason. If he has nothing to offer by way of amendment, he says:

S. W. to M. W. *(making the sign of a Master Mason.)* I have none, Worshipful Master.

W. M. to J. W. Have you any, brother Junior Warden?

J. W. to W. M. *(making the sign.)* None, Worshipful Master.

W. M. to Lodge. Has any brother around the Lodge any alterations to propose?

If none are offered the Master puts the question of

FELLOW CRAFT, OR SECOND DEGREE.

the adoption of the minutes, etc., then follows the other regular business of the Lodge, viz:

2. Reading and referring petitions.
3. Reports of Committees.
4. Balloting for Candidates.
5. Conferring Degrees.
6. Unfinished business.
7. Disposing of such other business as may lawfully come before the Lodge.

When the Master announces the fifth order of business *(conferring degrees)*, he proceeds as follows:

W. M. to J. D. Brother Junior Deacon, you will ascertain whether there are any candidates in waiting, and if so, who, and for what degree.

The Junior Deacon proceeds to the preparation room, and having ascertained that a candidate is there, reports as follows:

J. D. to W. M. Worshipful Master, brother A. B. is in waiting for the second degree.

The seventh and last order of business includes the work of initiation, passing and raising, and when all the other business of the Lodge has been transacted, the Master proceeds as follows:

W. M. Brethren, if there is no further business before this Lodge of Master Masons, we will proceed to close, and open a Lodge of Fellow Crafts for the purpose of passing brother A. B.

CALLING A LODGE FROM A HIGHER TO A LOWER DEGREE.

W. M. Brother Junior Warden, how goes the hour?

FELLOW CRAFT, OR SECOND DEGREE.

J. W. It is now high twelve, Worshipful Master.

W. M. It being high twelve, you will call the craft from labor to refreshment for the purpose of opening a Lodge of Fellow Crafts.

J. W. *(calls up the Lodge with three raps.)* Brethren, it is the will and pleasure of the Worshipful Master in the East that the Lodge be now called from labor to refreshment for the purpose of opening a Lodge of Fellow Crafts. Take notice and govern yourselves accordingly.—Look to the East!

W. M. Brethren, we are at refreshment. Brother Junior Deacon, inform the Tyler. Brother Senior Deacon, arrange the three Great Lights.

The Three Great Lights are closed. The Wardens reverse their columns, erect in the South, down in the East.

OPENING A LODGE OF FELLOW CRAFTS.

W. M. to S. W. Brother Senior Warden, proceed to satisfy yourself that all present are Fellow Crafts.

The Senior Warden rises and makes a personal observation of each person present. He then requests the Senior and Junior Deacons to give to him, in a whisper, the pass of a Fellow Craft and to demand it, under the same condition, from each person present except the Master, Senior Warden and Junior Warden. After this is done the Junior Deacon communicates the pass to the Senior Deacon and he to the Master.

W. M. to S. W. The pass is ——.

S. W. All present are Fellow Crafts.

The Master calls up the Senior and Junior Deacons by one rap.

FELLOW CRAFT, OR SECOND DEGREE.

W. M. to J. D. Brother Junior Deacon, what is the first great care of Masons when in Lodge assembled?

J. D. To see that the Lodge is duly tyled, Worshipful Master.

W. M. Perform that duty. Inform the Tyler that I am about to open a Lodge of Fellow Crafts, and direct him to tyle accordingly.

The Junior Deacon then goes to the door, opens it, and finding the Tyler at his post, duly armed, he communicates the Master's order and shuts the door.

J. D. to W. M. The Lodge is duly tyled, Worshipful Master.

W. M. How are we tyled, brother Junior Deacon?

J. D. By a brother Master Mason without the door, armed with the proper instrument of his office

W. M. What are his duties there?

J. D. To keep off all cowans and eavesdroppers. and to see that none pass or repass but such as are duly qualified and have permission from the Worshipful Master.

The Master seats the Deacons by one rap.

W. M. to S. W. Are you a Fellow Craft?

S. W. I am; try me.

W. M. How will you be tried?

S. W. By the Square.

W. M. Why by the Square?

S. W. Because it is one of the working tools of my profession.

After proceeding with such further portion of the lecture as he may see fit, the Master continues as follows:

FELLOW CRAFT, OR SECOND DEGREE.

W. M. to S. W. Where were you made a Fellow Craft?

S. W. In a just and lawfully constituted Lodge of Fellow Crafts.

W. M. How many anciently composed a Lodge of Fellow Crafts?

S. W. Five or more.

W. M. When composed of only five, who were they?

S. W. The Worshipful Master, Senior Warden, Junior Warden, Senior Deacon and Junior Deacon.

W. M. What is the Junior Deacon's place in the Lodge?

S. W. On the right side of the Senior Warden in the West.

W. M. to J. D. What are your duties there, brother Junior Deacon?

J. D. To carry messages from the Senior Warden in the West to the Junior Warden in the South, and elsewhere about the Lodge, as he may direct, and to see that the Lodge is duly tyled.

W. M. What is the Senior Deacon's place in the Lodge?

J. D. On the right of the Worshipful Master in the East.

W. M. to S. D. What are your duties there, brother Senior Deacon?

S. D. to W. M. To carry orders from the Worshipful Master in the East to the Senior Warden in the West, and elsewhere about the Lodge, as he may direct; to welcome and accommodate visiting brethren; to receive and conduct candidates.

FELLOW CRAFT, OR SECOND DEGREE.

W. M. to S. D. What is the Junior Warden's station in the Lodge.

S. D. In the South.

W. M. to J. W. Why are you in the South, brother Junior Warden? What are your duties there?

J. W. to W. M. As the Sun in the South at its meridian height is the glory and beauty of the day, so stands the Junior Warden in the South, the better to observe the time; to call the craft from labor to refreshment; to superintend them during the hours thereof, and see that they do not convert the purposes of refreshment into intemperance and excess; to call them on again in due season, that the Worshipful Master may have pleasure and the craft profit thereby.

W. M. o J. W. What is the Senior Warden's station in the Lodge?

J. W. In the West.

W. M. to S. W. Why are you in the West, brother Senior Warden? What are your duties there?

S. W. to W. M. As the Sun is in the West at the close of the day, so is the Senior Warden in the West to assist the Worshipful Master in opening and closing his Lodge; to pay the craft their wages, if any be due, and to see that none go away dissatisfied, harmony being the strength and support of all societies, more especially of ours.

W. M. to S. W. What is the Worshiful Master's station in the Lodge?

S. W. In the East.

W. M. Why is he in the East, brother Senior Warden? What are his duties there?

FELLOW CRAFT, OR SECOND DEGREE.

S. W. As the Sun rises in the East to open and govern the day, so rises the Worshipful Master in the East to open and govern his Lodge; to set the craft to work, and give them good and wholesome instruction for their labors.

The Master now calls up the Lodge by three raps, himself rising last.

W. M. to S. W. Brother Senior Warden, it is my will and pleasure that ———Lodge number———be now opened on the second degree of Masonry for the dispatch of such business as may regularly come before it, under the usual Masonic restrictions. Communicate this order to the Junior Warden in the South, and he to the craft for their government.

S. W. to J. W. Brother Junior Warden, it is the will and pleasure of the Worshipful Master in the East that ——— Lodge number ——— be now opened on the second degree of Masonry for the dispatch of such business as may regularly come before it, under the usual Masonic restrictions. Communicate this order to the craft for their government.

J. W. to Lodge. Brethren, it is the will and pleasure of the Worshipful Master in the East, communicated to me by the Senior Warden in the West, that ——— Lodge number ——— be now opened on the second degree of Masonry for the dispatch of such business as may regularly come before it, under the usual Masonic restrictions. Take notice and govern yourselves accordingly.—Look to the East!

The craft now face the Master, and with him make, slowly and carefully, the signs of an Entered Apprentice and Fellow Craft. After the signs are

FELLOW CRAFT, OR SECOND DEGREE.

given, the Junior Warden gives one rap, followed by the Senor Warden and the Worshipful Master. These raps are passed about twice.

After the usual prayer, the Worshipful Master proceeds:

W. M. to Lodge. In the name of God and the Holy Saints John, I declare ——— Lodge number ——— opened in form on the second degree. Brother Junior Deacon, inform the Tyler.

The Master seats the Lodge by one rap. The Junior Deacon repairs to the door and knocks thrice upon it, when it is opened by the Tyler, to whom the Junior Deacon announces that the Lodge is opened upon the second degree. He then shuts the door, which is locked upon the outside by the Tyler.

J. D. to W. M. The duty is performed, Worshipful Master.

The Master seats the Deacon by one rap.

Meanwhile, the Senior Deacon arranges the three Great Lights duly upon the altar, the Bible laying open at Amos VII, and one point of the compasses underneath the square. The Wardens reverse their columns, erect in the West, down in the South.

The Lodge is now duly open in the Fellow Craft degree, for the purpose of passing an Entered Apprentice.

CEREMONIES OF PASSING.

W. M. Brother Stewards, you will repair to the preparation room, where you will find brother A. B. in waiting, whom you will duly prepare for passing to the second degree of Masonry.

FELLOW CRAFT, OR SECOND DEGREE.

The Stewards step to the altar, make the proper sign, and leaving the altar on their right proceed to the preparation room.

After the customary questions have been put by the Stewards and duly answered by the candidate, they prepare him in the manner laid down for this degree, the candidate wearing his apron as an Entered Apprentice. They then conduct him to the door of the Lodge, on which they require him to make three distinct knocks.

When these are heard in the Lodge the Senior Deacon rises from his seat, and says:

S. D. Worshipful Master, there is an alarm at the door of the preparation room.

W. M. to S. D. Attend to the alarm.

The Senior Deacon, leaving the altar on his right, proceeds to the door of the preparation room, and answers the alarm by three similar knocks on the door, which is then opened by the Stewards just enough to admit of conversation.

S. D. Who comes here?

Steward. A brother who has been regularly initiated as an Entered Apprentice, and now wishes to receive more light in Masonry by being passed to the degree of a Fellow Craft.

S. D. to Candidate. Is is of your own free will and accord?

Candidate. It is.

S. D. to Steward. Is he duly and truly prepared?

Steward. He is.

S. D. Is he worthy and well qualified?

Steward. He is.

FELLOW CRAFT, OR SECOND DEGREE.

S. D. Has he made suitable proficiency in the preceding degree?

Steward. He has.

S. D. By what further right or benefit does he expect to gain admittance?

Steward. By the benefit of the pass.

S. D. Has he the pass?

Steward. He has not; I have it for him.

S. D. Give me the pass.

The door is opened just sufficient for the Steward to give the pass in a low whisper to the Senior Deacon.

S. D. Let him wait with patience until the Worshipful Master is informed of his request and his answer returned.

The Senior Deacon closes the door, proceeds to the altar, where he salutes the Master, and then gives three knocks on the floor with his rod.

W. M. Who comes there?

S. D. A brother who has been regularly initiated as an Entered Apprentice, and now wishes to receive more light in Masonry by being passed to the degree of a Fellow Craft.

W. M. Is it of his own free will and accord?

S. D. It is.

W. M. Is he duly and truly prepared?

S. D. He is.

W. M. Is he worthy and well qualified?

S. D. He is.

W. M. Has he made suitable proficiency in the preceding degree?

S. D. He has.

FELLOW CRAFT, OR SECOND DEGREE.

W. M. Since he comes endowed with all these essential qualifications, it is my will and pleasure that he enter this Lodge of Fellow Crafts, and that you receive him in due and ancient form.

The Senior Deacon returns to the door of the preparation room, opens it wide, and says to the Steward:

S. D. It is the will and pleasure of the Worshipful Master that he enter this Lodge of Fellow Crafts.

The Stewards conduct the candidate between them into the Lodge, and, after closing the door behind them, they salute and take their seats.

The Senior Deacon places his left hand upon the Candidate's right shoulder and says:

S. D. to Candidate. My brother, it is the will and pleasure of the Worshipful Master that I receive you into this Lodge of Fellow Crafts in due and ancient form. You are received on the angle of the Square at your naked right breast; which is to teach you that the Square of virtue should be a rule and guide to your conduct in all your future action with mankind.

The Senior Deacon now takes the candidate's right hand in his own left hand, and conducts him with slow and measured steps in a direct line nearly to the North-east corner of the Lodge, and turning at right angles, thence to near the South-east corner; thence to the South-west corner and thence back to near the North-west corner.

The same circuit is then repeated.

On their first circuit about the Lodge, as they pass the Master's, Senior Warden's and Junior Warden's

FELLOW CRAFT, OR SECOND DEGREE.

stations respectively, each of those officers give one rap. On their second circuit each officer greets their passage by two raps. During their progerss the Master reads from the seventh chapter of Amos, commencing to read at the first rap given by the Junior Warden, and timing it so as to finish reading at the end of the march.

The Senior Deacon then conducts the candidate in front of the Junior Warden's station in the South, one pace distant, where he gives three knocks on the floor with his rod.

J. W. Who comes there?

S. D. A brother who has been regularly initiated as an Entered Appretice, and now wishes to receive more light in Masonry by being passed to the degree of a Fellow Craft.

J. W. to Candidate. Is it of your own free will and accord?

Candidate. It is,

J. W. to S. D. Is he duly and truly prepared?

S. D. He is.

J. W. Is he worthy and well qualified.

S. D. He is.

J. W. Has he made suitable proficiency in the preceding degree?

S. D. He has.

J. W. By what further right or benefit does he expect to gain admission?

S. D. By the benefit of the pass.

J. W. Has he the pass?

S. D. He has not; I have it for him.

J. W. Advance and give it.

FELLOW CRAFT, OR SECOND DEGREE.

The Senior Deacon advances and gives the pass.

J. W. to S. D. Conduct the candidate to the Senior Warden in the West for further examination.

The Senior Deacon and candidate then pass on to the Senior Warden's station in the West, where the three knocks are repeated, and the same questions are asked and answers returned as at the Junior Warden's station.

S. W. to S. D. Conduct the candidate to the Worshipful Master in the East, for final examination.

The two then proceed to the Master's station in the East, and the same knocks, questions and answers are repated as before.

W. M. to Candidate. You will be reconducted to the Senior Warden in the West, who will teach you how to approach to the East by two upright, regular steps, your feet forming the right angle of an oblong square, your body erect to the Worshipful Master in the East.

The Senior Deabon obeys the order, leaving the altar on his right as he does so.

S. D. to S. W. Brother Senior Warden, it is the will and pleasure of the Worshipful Master in the East that this brother be taught to approach to the East, advancing by two upright, regular steps, his feet forming the right angle of an oblong square, his body erect to the worshipful Master in the East.

S. W. to S. D. You will see that the Worshipful Masters orders are obeyed.

The Senior Deacon now causes the candidate to face to the East, and instructs him how to take the proper steps as follows:

FELLOW CRAFT, OR SECOND DEGREE.

S. D. to Candidate. You will face to the East. step off with your left foot as an Entered Apprentice; now take another step with your right foot, bringing the heel of the left foot to the hollow of the right, your feet forming the right angle of an oblong square. Stand erect!

S. D. to W. M. Your orders have been obeyed, Worshipful Master.

While the candidate is in this position, the Master addresses the candidate from the chair as follows:

W. M. to Candidate. My brother, Masonry is a progressive science, and as we advance in knowledge, our obligations to ourselves and to our brethren correspondingly increase. As an Entered Apprentice you were simply bound to secrecy, while the holy principles of morality and virtue were inculcated by beautiful ceremonies and lectures. As a Fellow Craft, your obligations will be greatly extended; and like the others, they can never be repudiated or laid aside. Yet, as before, I am free to inform you that these new obligations, like those you have heretofore taken, contain nothing which can conflict with your duty to God, your country, your neighbor or yourself. With this renewed pledge on my part, as the Master of the Lodge, I ask you, are you willing to take such an obligation, as all Masons have done before you?

The candidate assenting, the Master proceeds:

W. M. to S. D. Place the candidate in due form to be made a Fellow Craft.

S. D. to Candidate. Advance! Kneel on your

FELLOW CRAFT, OR SECOND DEGREE.

naked right knee, your left forming a square. Your body erect, your naked right hand resting on the Holy Bible, square and compasses, your left elbow forming a right angle, supported by the square.

With each direction, the Senior Deacon places the candidate in a corresponding position.

S. D. to W. M. The candidate is in due form, Worshipful Master.

The Master now calls up the Lodge by three raps. He rises last, uncovers his head, goes to and stands erect before the altar, and places his right hand on the Holy Bible.

W. M. to Candidate. You will repeat your name and say after me:

I, A. B., of my own free will and accord, in the presence of Almighty God and this worshipful Lodge, erected to Him and dedicated to the Holy Saints John, do hereby and hereon most solemnly and sincerely promise and swear, as I have heretofore done, but with these additions:

That I will not communicate the secrets of a Fellow Craft to an Entered Apprentice nor those of an Entered Apprentice to the rest of the world, neither these nor any of them to any person or persons whatsoever, except it be to a true and lawful brother Mason, or within the body of a just and lawfully constituted Lodge of Masons; nor unto him or them until by strict trial, due examination, or lawful information, I shall have found him or them as lawfully entitled to them as I am myself.

I furthermore promise and swear that I will stand to and abide by all the laws, rules and regulations

FELLOW CRAFT, OR SECOND DEGREE.

of a Fellow Craft Lodge, so far as they shall come to my knowledge.

I furthermore promise and swear that I will answer and obey all due signs and summonses sent me from a Lodge of Fellow Crafts, or handed me by a brother of this degree, if within the limits of my cable-tow.

I furthermore promise and swear that I will help, aid and assist all poor, distressed brother Fellow Crafts, they applying to me as such and I deeming them worthy.

I furthermore promise and swear that I will not cheat, wrong or defraud a Lodge of Fellow Crafts, or a brother of this degree, knowingly or wittingly.

All this I most solemnly and sincerely promise and swear, with a firm and steadfast resolution to keep and perform the same, without the least equivocation, mental reservation or self-evasion whatsoever; binding myself under no less penalty than that of having my left breast torn open, my heart plucked from thence, and given to the beasts of the field and the birds of air as a prey, should I, in the least, knowingly or wittingly, violate or transgress this my Fellow Craft obligation. So help me God and keep me steadfast.

W. M. to Candidate. In token of your sincerity of purpose in this solemn engagement, you will kiss the Holy Bible, now open before you.

The candidate kisses the Bible.

W. M. to S. D. Brother Senior Deacon, our brother being again bound to us by a covenant which cannot be broken, you will release him from his cable-tow.

FELLOW CRAFT, OR SECOND DEGREE.

This order is obeyed.

W. M. to Candidate. My brother, for by that sacred appellation I again address you ,in your present blind condition, what do you most desire?

Candidate *(prompted by the Senior Deacon)*. More light in Masonry.

W. M. to Candidate. More light being your desire, you shall receive it.

W. M. to Lodge. My brethren, you will again stretch forth your hands and assist me in bringing this brother to more light in Masonry.

All the brethren, except the Wardens, now come forward and form two parallel lines from East to West.

W. M. In the beginning God created the heavens and the earth. And the earth was without form and void; and darkness was upon the face of the deep. And the spirit of God moved upon the face of the waters. And God said, Let there be light, and there was light. In solemn commemoration of that sublime event, I, in like manner, Masonically declare, Let there be light!

At the word "light," all present strike their hands forcibly together once and stamp with their right feet, and at the same instant the Senior Deacon removes the hoodwink.

W. M. and there is light!

W. M. to Candidate. My brother, on being brought to light, you discover on the altar before you more than you have heretofore done; one point of the compasses bare, the other being hidden; which is to each you that as yet you have received light in Masonry but partially.

FELLOW CRAFT, OR SECOND DEGREE.

The Master now retires to the East and advancing, says:

W. M. to Candidate. You now discover me approaching from the East under the due guard *(makes due guard)* and sign *(makes sign)* of a Fellow Craft. In token of the continuance of my brotherly love and favor, I again present you with my right hand, and with it the pass, token of the pass, grip and word of a Fellow Craft *(gives them)*. Arise! Salute the Wardens as a Fellow Craft.

The Master returns to his station in the East, and seats himself and the Lodge by one rap. The Senior Deacon conducts the candidate to the Junior Warden's station in the South, leaving the altar on the right, and the candidate salutes the Junior Warden with the due guard and sign of a Fellow Craft. They then pass to the Senior Warden's station in the West, and the candidate salutes him in the same manner; and lastly they go to the West of the altar, and the candidate salutes the Master as he did the Wardens.

W. M. to Candidate. My brother, you will now be reconducted to the Senior Warden in the West, who will teach you how to wear your apron as a Fellow Craft.

The Senior Deacon conducts the candidate to the Senior Warden, and says:

S. D. to S. W. Brother Senior Warden, it is the will and pleasure of the Worshipful Master in the East that our newly admitted brother be taught how to wear his apron as a Fellow Craft.

S. W. to S. D. You will see that the orders of the Worshipful Master are obeyed.

FELLOW CRAFT, OR SECOND DEGREE.

The candidate is invested by the Senior Deacon, who then conducts him to the right hand of the Master in the East.

W. M. to Candidate. I now present you with the working tools of a Fellow Craft. They are the Plumb, Square and Level.

The Plumb is an instrument made use of by operative masons to raise perpendiculars; the Square to square their work; and the Level to lay horizontals, but we, as Free and Accepted Masons, are taught to make use of them for more noble and glorious purposes.

The Plumb admonishes us to walk uprightly in our several stations before God and man, squaring our actions by the square of Virtue, and remembering that we are traveling upon the Level of Time to that undiscovered country from whose bourne no traveler returns.

You will now be reconducted to the place from whence you came, and there be re-invested of what you were divested; after which, agreeable to an ancient custom in all regular and well governed Lodges of Fellow Crafts, it will be necessary that you make a regular ascent up a flight of winding stairs, consisting of three, five and seven steps, into a place representing the middle chamber of King Solomon's Temple, there to receive further instruction relative to the wages of a Fellow Craft, which are corn, wine and oil, emblematical of peace, unity and plenty.

The candidate is now conducted to the altar, where he is instructed to salute the Master; he is

FELLOW CRAFT, OR SECOND DEGREE.

then taken to the preparation room, and placed in charge of the Stewards, where he resumes his regular apparel.

While he is thus occupied, the columns, which represent the pillars of the porch of King Solomon's Temple, are placed upright near the door of the preparation room, so as to leave a space of about four feet between the columns. A floor-cloth, on which are represented the three, five and seven steps, is laid on the floor, so as to lead from the columns around the altar, and up to the Junior Warden's station in the South. When the candidate returns to the Lodge, the Senior Deacon meets him at the door of the preparation room, and placing him between the columns, says:

S. D. to Candidate. My brother, you were informed by the Worshipful Master that, agreeable to an ancient custom in all regular and well-governed Lodge of Fellow Crafts, it is necessary that you make a regular ascent up a flight of winding stairs, consisting of three, five and seven steps, into a place representing the middle chamber of King Solomon's Temple, there to receive further instruction relative to the wages of a Fellow Craft, which are corn, wine and oil, emblematical of peace, unity and plenty.

In pursuance of his orders, I proceed to conduct you to the middle chamber.

There are two kinds of Masonry, operative and speculative.

By operative Masonry we allude to a proper application of the useful rules of architecture, whence

FELLOW CRAFT, OR SECOND DEGREE.

a structure will derive figure, strength and beauty, and whence will result a due proportion and a just correspondence in all its parts. It furnishes us with dwellings and convenient shelter from the vicissitudes and inclemencies of the seasons; and while it displays the effects of human wisdom, as well in the choice as in the arrangement of the sundry materials of which an edifice is composed, it demonstrates that a fund of science and industry is implanted in man for the best, most salutary and beneficent purposes.

By speculative Masonry we learn to subdue the passions, act upon the square, keep a tongue of good report, maintain secrecy and practice charity. It is so far interwoven with religion as to lay us under obligations to pay that rational homage to the Deity which at once constitutes our duty and our happiness. It leads the contemplative to view with reverence and admiration the glorious works of the creation, and inspres him with the most elated ideas of the perfections of his Divine Creator.

We work as speculative Masons only; but our ancient brethren worked in operative as well as speculative Masonry. They worked six days and received their wages. They did not work on the seventh day, because in six days God created the heavens and the earth, and rested upon the seventh day. The seventh, therefore, our ancient brethren consecrated as a day of rest from their labors, thereby enjoying frequent opportunities to contemplate the glorious works of the creation and to adore their great Creator.

FELLOW CRAFT, OR SECOND DEGREE.

In conducting you into a place representing the middle chamber of King Solomon's Temple, you will observe various objects that will particularly attract your attention. These two great pillars, the one on the right hand, the other on the left, are called Jachin and Boaz. The word Boaz denotes strength. The word Jachin denotes establishment. These names collectively allude to the promise of God to David, that he would establish his kingdom in strength. These pillars were cast in the claygrounds on the banks of Jordan, between Succoth and Zarthan, where all the vessels of King Solomon's Temple were cast by Hiram Abiff. They were cast hollow the better to serve as a safe deposit for the archives of Masonry against all conflagrations and inundations.

They were each thirty-five cubits in height, and were adorned with chapiters of five cubits, making in all forty cubits in height. These were adorned with lily-work, network and pomegranates, representing peace, unity and plenty.

The Lily, by its purity and the retired situation in which it grows, denotes Peace; the Network, by the intimate connection of its parts, denotes Unity; the Pomegranates, by the exuberance of their seed, denote Plenty.

The two pillars were further adorned with globes on their tops, representing the terrestrial and celestial spheres. The globes are two artificial spherical bodies, on the convex surface of which are represented the countries, seas and various parts of the earth, the face of the heavens, the planetary revolu-

FELLOW CRAFT, OR SECOND DEGREE.

tions, and other particulars. The sphere with the parts of the earth delineated on its surface is called the terrestrial globe, and that with the constellations and other heavenly bodies the celestial globe.

The principal use of the globes, besides serving as maps to distinguish the outward parts of the earth and the situation of the fixed stars, is to illustrate and explain the phenomena arising from the annual revolution and the diurnal rotation of the earth around its own axis. They are the noblest instruments for improving the mind and giving it the most distinct idea of any problem or proposition, as well as enabling it to solve the same.

Contemplating these bodies, we are inspired with a due reverence for the Deity and His works, and are induced to encourage the study of astronomy, geometry, navigation and the arts dependent on them, by which society has been so much benefied. The globes also denote the uneversality of Masonry.

After passing the pillars, we next arrive at a flight of winding stairs, consisting of three, five and seven steps. The number three alludes to the first three degrees of Masonry, and also to the three principal officers of the Lodge. *(They pass over the three steps.)* The five steps allude to the five orders of architecture. By order in architecture is meant a system of all the members, proportions and ornaments of columns and pilasters. Or it is a regular arrangement of the projecting parts of a building, which, united with those of a column, form a beautiful, perfect and complete work.

From the first formation of society order in archi-

FELLOW CRAFT, OR SECOND DEGREE.

tecture may be traced. When the rigor of seasons obliged men to contrive shelter from the inclemency of the weather, we learn that they first planted trees on end, and then laid others across, to support a covering. The bands which connected those trees at the top and bottom are said to have given rise to the idea of the base and capital of pillars, and from this simple hint originally proceeded the more improved art of architecture.

The five orders are thus classed: The Tuscan, Doric, Ionic, Corinthian and Composite. The Tuscan is the most simple and solid of the five orders. It was invented in Tuscany, whence it derived its name. Its column is seven diameters high, and its capital, base and entablature have but few moldings. The simplicity of the construction of this column renders it eligible where ornament would be superfluous. The Doric, which is plain and natural, is the most ancient, and was invented by the Greeks. Its column is eight diameters high, and has seldom any ornaments on base or capital except moldings; though the frieze is distinguished by triglyphs and metopes, and triglyphs compose the ornaments of the frieze. The solid composition of this order gives it a preference in structures where strength and a noble simplicity are chiefly required. The Doric is the best proportioned of all the orders. The several parts of which it is composed are founded on the natural position of solid bodies. In its first invention it was more simple than in its present state. In after times, when it began to be adorned, it gained the name of Doric; for when it was constructed in its primitive and simple form, the name of Tuscan was conferred on it. Hence the Tuscan precedes the Doric in rank, on account of its resemblance to that pillar in its original state. The Ionic bears a kind of mean proportion between the more solid and delicate orders. Its column is nine diameters high, its capital is adorned with volutes and its corners hasdentals. There is both delicacy and ingenuity displayed in this pillar, the invention of which is attributed to the Ionians, as the famous temple of Diana at Ephesus was of this order. It is said to have been formed after the model of an agreeable young woman of an elegant shape, dressed in her hair, as a contrast to the Doric order, which was formed after that of a strong, robust man. The Corinthian, the richest of the five orders, is deemed a masterpiece of art. Its column is ten diameters high, and its capital is adorned with two rows of leaves, and eight volutes, which sustain the abacus. The frieze is ornamented with curious devices, the corners with dentals and modillions. This order is used in stately and superb structures. It was invented at Corinth, by Callimachus, who is said to have taken the hint of the capital of this pillar from the following remarkable circumstance: Accidentally passing by the tomb of a young lady, he perceived a basket of toys, covered with a tile, placed over an acanthus root, having been left there by her nurse. As the branches grew up, they encompassed the basket, till, arriving at the tile, they met with an obstruction and bent downward. Callimachus, struck with the object, set about imitating the figure; the vase of the capital he made to represent the basket, the abacus the tile, and the volutes the bending leaves. The Composite is compounded of the other orders, and was contrived by the Romans. Its capital has the two rows of leaves of the Corinthian and the volutes of the Ionic. Its column has the quarter-round, as the Tuscan and Doric order, is ten diameters high, and its corners has dentals, or simple modillions. This pillar is generally found in buildings where strength, elegance and beauty are displayed.

The ancient and original orders of architecture, revered by Masons, are no more than three, the Doric, Ionic and Corinthian, which were invented by the Greeks. To these the Romans have added two: the Tuscan, which they made plainer than the Doric; and the Composite, which was more ornamental, if not more beautiful, than the Corinthian. The first three orders alone, however, show invention and particular character, and essentially differ from each other; the two others have nothing but what is borrowed, and differ only accidentally. The Tuscan is the Doric in its earliest state, and the Composite is the Corinthian enriched with the Ionic. To the Greeks, therefore, and not to the Romans, we are indebted for what is great, judicious and distinct in architecture.

The five steps also allude to the five senses of human nature. These are hearing, seeing, feeling, smelling and tasting. Hearing is that sense by which we distinguish sounds, and are capable of enjoying all the agreeable charms of music. By it we are enabled to enjoy the pleasures of society, and reciprocally to communicate to each other our thoughts and intentions, our purposes and desires, while thus our reason is capable of exerting its utmost power and energy. The wise and beneficent Author of Nature intended, by the formation of this sense, that we should be social creatures, and receive the greatest and most important part of our knowledge by the information of others. For these purposes we are endowed with hearing, that, by a proper exertion of our natural powers, our happiness may be complete. Seeing is that sense by which we distinguish objects, and, in an instant of time, without change of place or situation, view armies in battle array, figures of the most stately structures, and all the agreeable variety displayed in the landscape of nature. By this sense we find our way in the pathless ocean, traverse the globe of earth, determine its figure and dimensions, and delineate any region or quarter of it. By it we measure the planetary orbs and make new discoveries in the sphere of the fixed stars. Nay, more, by it we perceive the tempers and dispositions, the passions and affections of our fellow-creatures when they wish most to conceal them; so that though the tongue may be taught to lie and dissemble, the countenance would display hypocrisy to the discerning eye. In fine, the rays of light which administer to this sense are the most astonishing parts of the animated creation, and render the eye a peculiar object of admiration. Of all the faculties, sight is the noblest. The structure of the eye and its appurtenances evinces

FELLOW CRAFT, OR SECOND DEGREE.

the admirable contrivance of nature for performing all its various external and internal motions; while the variety displayed in the eyes of different animals, suited to their several ways of life, clearly demonstrates this organ to be the masterpiece of nature's work. Feeling is that sense by which we distinguish the different qualities of bodies, such as heat and cold, hardness and softness, roughness and smoothnass, figure, solidity, motion and extension. These three senses, hearing, seeing and feeling, are most revered by Masons, because by the sense of hearing we distinguish the word; by that of seeing, we perceive the sign; and by that of feeling, we receive the grip, whereby one Mason may know another in the dark as well as in the light.

Smelling is that sense by which we distinguish odors, the various kinds of which convey different opinions to the mind. Animal and vegetable bodies, and, indeed, most other bodies, while exposed to the air, continually send forth effluvia of vast subtilty, as well in the state of life and growth as in the state of fermentation and putrefaction. These effluvia, being drawn into the nostrils along with the air, are the means by which all bodies are smelled. Hence, it is evident that there is a manifest appearance of design in the great Creator's having planted the organ of smell in the inside of that canal through which the air continually passes in respiration. Tasting enables us to make a proper distinction in the choice of our food. The organ of this sense guards the entrance of the alimentary canal, as that of smelling guards the entrance of the canal

FELLOW CRAFT, OR SECOND DEGREE.

for respiration. From the situation of both these organs, it is plain that they were intended by nature to distinguish wholesome food from that which is nauseous. Everything that enters into the stomach must undergo the scrutiny of tasting; and by it we are capable of discerning the changes which the same body undegoes in the different compositions of art, cookery, chemistry, pharmacy, &c.

Smelling and tasting are inseparably connected, and it is by the unnatural kind of life men commonly lead in society that these senses are rendered less fit to perform their natural offices.

On the mind all our knowledge must depend. What, therefore, can be a more proper subject for the investigation of Masons? By anatomical dissection and observation we become acquainted with the body; but it is by the anatomy of the mind alone we discover its powers and principles.

To sum up the whole of this transcendent measure of God's bounty to man, we shall add that memory, imagination, taste, reasoning, moral perception, and all the active powers of the soul, present a vast and boundless field for philosophical disquisition, which far exceed human inquiry, and are peculiar mysteries, known only to nature and to nature's God, to whom we are all indebted for creation, preservation and every blessing we enjoy.

(They pass over the five steps.)

The number seven alludes to the seven liberal arts and sciences:—grammar, rhetoric, logic, arithmetic, geometry, music and astronomy. Grammar teaches the proper arrangement of words according to the

FELLOW CRAFT, OR SECOND DEGREE.

idiom or dialect of any particular people, and that excellency of pronunciation which enables us to speak or write a language with accuracy, agreeable to reason and correct usage. Rhetoric teaches us to speak copiously and fluently on any subject, not merely with propriety alone, but with all the advantages of force and elegance; wisely contriving to captivate the hearer by strength of argument and beauty of expression, whether it be to entreat or exhort, to admonish or applaud. Logic teaches us to guide our reason discretionally in the general knowledge of things, and directs our inquiries after truth. It consists of a regular train of argument, whence we infer, deduce and conclude, according to certain premises laid down, admitted or granted; and in it are employed the faculties of conceiving, judging, reasoning and disposing, all of which are naturally led on from one gradation to another, till the point in question is finally determined. Arithmetic teaches the powers and properties of numbers, which is variously effected by letters, tables, figures and instruments. By this art, reasons and demonstrations are given for finding out any certain number whose relation or affinity to another is already known or discovered. Geometry treats of the powers and properties of magnitudes in general, where length, breadth and thickness are considered, from a point to a line, from a line to a superficies, and from a superficies to a solid. A point is a dimensionless figure on an indivisible part of space. A line is a point continued, and a figure of one capacity, namely, length. A superficies is a figure of two di-

FELLOW CRAFT, OR SECOND DEGREE.

mensions, namely, length and breadth. A solid is a figure of three dimensions, namely, length, breadth and thickness. By this science the architect is enabled to construct his plans and execute his designs; the general to arrange his soldiers; the engineer to mark out ground for encampments; the geographer to give us the dimensions of the world and all things therein contained, to delineate the extent of seas and specify the divisions of empires, kingdoms and provinces. By it, also, the astronomer is enabled to make his observations, and to fix the durations of times and seasons, years and cycles. In fine, geometry is the foundation of architecture and the root of the mathematics. Music teaches the art of forming concords, so as to compose delightful harmony by a mathematical and proportional arrangement of acute, grave and mixed sounds. This art, by a series of experiments, is reduced to a demonstrative science, with respect to tones and the intervals of sound. It inquires into the nature of concords and discords, and enables us to find out the proportion between them by numbers. Astronomy is that divine art by which we are taught to read the wisdom, strength and beauty of the Almighty Creator in those sacred pages, the celestial hemisphere. Assisted by astronomy, we can observe the motions, measure the distances, comprehend the magnitudes, and calculate the periods and eclipses of the heavenly bodies. By it we learn the use of the globes, the system of the world, and the preliminary law of nature. While we are employed in the study of this science, we must perceive unparalleled in-

FELLOW CRAFT, OR SECOND DEGREE.

stances of wisdom and goodness, and, through the whole creation, trace the glorious Author by His works.

By this time they have arrived at the Junior Warden's station in the South. The Senior Deacon gives three knocks upon the floor with his rod.

J. W. to S. D. Who comes here?

S. D. to J. W. A Fellow Craft on his way to the middle chamber.

J. W. How does he expect to gain admission?

S. D. By the pass and the token of the pass of a Fellow Craft.

J. W. Give me the pass.

S. D. *Gives the pass.*

S. D. Plenty.

J. W. How is it represented?

S. D. By an ear of corn hanging near a waterford.

J. W. From whence originated this word?

S. D. In consequence of a quarrel between Jephtha, judge of Israel, and the Ephraimites, the Ephraimites having long been a turbulent and rebellious people, whom Jephtha sought to overcome by lenient measures, but without effect. They being highly enraged at not being invited to fight and share in the rich spoils of the Ammonitish war, gathered together a mighty army; Jephtha also gathered together all the men of Gilead, gave them battle and put them to flight. And in order to make his victory more complete, he placed guards at the several passes of Jordan, and commanded that if any should attempt to pass that way, to demand of

FELLOW CRAFT, OR SECOND DEGREE.

them, say now Sh————. But they, being of a different tribe, could not frame to pronounce it right, and said S————. This they did proving themselves enemies, and it cost them their lives. And there fell at that time of the Ephraimites forty and two thousand. Since which time this word has been adopted as a regular word to gain admission into all regular and well governed Lodges of Fellow Crafts.

J. W. Give me the token of the pass.

S. D. *Gives the token of the pass.*

J. W. Your pass and token of the pass are correct. You may now pass on through the outer door of the middle chamber.

S. D. My brother, we are now approaching a place representing the inner door to the middle chamber, which we shall find guarded by the Senior Warden.

They pass around the Junior Warden's station and proceed to the Senior Warden's station in the West. Upon arriving there the Senior Deacon gives three knocks upon the floor with his rod.

S. W. to S. D. Who comes here?

S. D. to S. W. A Fellow Craft on his way to the middle chamber.

S. W. How does he expect to gain admission?

S. D. By the grip and word of a Fellow Craft.

The Senior Deacon gives them, and then follow five questions and answers which refer solely to the grip, etc.

S. W. Your grip and word are correct. You may pass within the inner door.

FELLOW CRAFT, OR SECOND DEGREE.

They now pass on to the Worshipful Master in the East, and on arriving there the Senior Deacon gives three knocks as before.

W. M. to S. D. Who comes here?

S. D. to W. M. A Fellow Craft desirous to receive his wages.

W. M. to Candidate. My brother, you have been admitted into the middle chamber by virtue of the letter G, that you might receive your wages. At the building of King Solomon's Temple the Fellow Crafts were paid in wages consisting of corn, wine and oil. We, as speculative Masons only, receive as wages the emblematical corn of nourishment, the wine of refreshment, and the oil of joy. *(To Secretary.)* Brother Secretary, you will record the name of brother A. B. as a Fellow Craft, entitling him to all the wages of speculative Masonry. *(To Candidate.)* My brother, I said you had been admitted into the middle chamber by virtue of the letter G. It is universally displayed over the Master's chair, as you here discover. It is the initial of geometry. Geometry, the first and noblest of sciences, is the basis on which the superstructure of Masonry is erected. By geometry we may curiously trace Nature through her various windings to her most concealed recesses. By it we discover the power, the wisdom and the goodness of the Grand Artificer of the Universe, and view with delight the proportions which connect this vast machine. By it we discover how the planets move in their different orbits and demonstrate their various revolutions. By it we account for the return of seasons and the variety of

FELLOW CRAFT, OR SECOND DEGREE.

scenes which each season displays to the discerning eye. Numberless worlds are around us, all framed by the same Divine Artist, which roll through the vast expanse, and are all conducted by the same unerring law of nature.

A survey of nature, and the observations of her beautiful proportions, first determined men to imitate the Divine plan, and study symmetry and order. This gave rise to societies and birth to every useful art. The architect began to design, and the plans which he laid down, being improved by experience and time, have produced works which are the admiration of every age.

The lapse of time, the ruthless hand of ignorance, and the devastations of war have laid waste and destroyed many valuable monuments of antiquity on which the utmost exertions of human genius have been employed. Even the Temple of Solomon, so spacious and magnificent, and constructed by so many celebrated artists, escaped not the unsparing ravages of barbarous force. Freemasonry, notwithstanding, has still survived. The attentive ear receives the sound from the instructive tongue, and the mysteries of Masonry are safely lodged in the repository of faithful breasts. Tools and implements of architecture are selected by the fraternity to imprint on the memory wise and serious truths; and thus, through a succession of ages, are transmitted unimpaired the excellent tenets of our institution.

The letter G also alludes to the sacred name of Deity, *(the Master uncovers and calls up the Lodge)* before whom we should all, from the youngest En-

FELLOW CRAFT, OR SECOND DEGREE.

tered Apprentice in the North-east corner to the Worshipful Master who presides in the East, with reverence most humbly bow. *(Here all make a solemn obeisance.)*

The Master then delivers the following charge:

W. M. to Candidate. Brother, being advanced to the second degree of Masonry, we congratulate you on your preferment. The internal and not the external qualifications of a man are what Masonry regards. As you increase in knowledge you will improve in social intercourse. It is unnecessary to recapitulate the duties which, as a Mason, you are bound to discharge, or enlarge on the necessity of a strict adherence to them, as your own experience must have established their value.

Our laws and regulations you are strenuously to support, and be always ready to assist in duly enforcing them. You are not to palliate or aggravate the offenses of your brethren; but in the decision of every trespass against our rules, you are to judge with candor, admonish with friendship, and reprehend with justice.

The study of the liberal arts, that valuable branch of education which tends so effectually to polish and adorn the mind, is earnestly recommended to your consideration, especially the science of geometry, which is established as the basis of our art. Geometry, or Masonry, originally synonymous terms, being of a divine and moral nature, is enriched with the most useful knowledge; while it proves the wonderful properties of nature, it demonstrates the more important truths of morality.

FELLOW CRAFT, OR SECOND DEGREE.

Your past behavior and regular deportment have merited the honor which we have now conferred and in your new character it is expected that you will conform to the principles of the Order by perserverance in the practice of every commendable virtue.

Such is the nature of your engagement as a Fellow Craft, and to these duties you are sacredly bound.

The Master then seats the Lodge, directs the newly passed brother to a seat in front, and rehearses the entire two sections of the lecture. When this is concluded the brother is directed to seat himself among the other brethren.

LECTURE OF THE SECOND DEGREE.
Second Degree.

W. M. Will you be off or from?

S. W. From.

W. M. From what to what?

S. W. From the degree of an Entered Apprentice to that of a Fellow Craft.

W. M. Are you a Fellow Craft?

S. W. I am; try me.

W. M. How will you be tried?

S. W. By the square.

W. M. Why by the square?

S. W. Because it is an emblem of morality and one of the working tools of a Fellow Craft.

W. M. What is a square?

S. W. An angle of ninety degrees, or the fourth part of a circle.

FELLOW CRAFT, OR SECOND DEGREE.

W. M. Where were you made a Fellow Craft?

S. W. In a just and lawfully constituted Lodge of Fellow Crafts.

W. M. How were you prepared?

S. W. By being divested of all metals, neither naked nor clothed, barefoot nor shod, hoodwinked, and a cable-tow twice about my naked right arm; in which situation I was conducted to the door of the Lodge by a brother.

W. M. Why had you a cable-tow twice about your naked right arm?

S. W. It was to signify that as a Fellow Craft I was under a double tie to the fraternity.

W. M. How gained you admission?

S. W. By three distinct knocks.

W. M. To what do those knocks allude?

S. W. To the three jewels of a Fellow Craft: the attentive ear. the instructive tongue and the faithful breast.

W. M. What was said to you from within?

S. W. Who comes here?

W. M. Your answer?

S. W. A brother who has been regularly initiated as an Entered Apprentice ,and now wishes to receive more light in Masonry by being passed to the degree of a Fellow Craft.

W. M. What were you then asked?

S. W. If it was of my own free will and accord; if I was duly and truly prepared; worthy and well qualified; if I had made suitable proficiency in the preceding degree; all of which being answered in the affirmative, I was asked by what further right or benefit I expected to gain admission.

FELLOW CRAFT, OR SECOND DEGREE.

W. M. Your answer?
S. W. By the benefit of the pass.
W. M. Did you give the pass?
S. W. I gave it not; my guide gave it for me.
W. M. What followed?
S. W. I was directed to wait with patience until the Worshipful Master was informed of my request and his answer returned.
W. M. What answer did he return?
S. W. Let him enter and be received in due form.
W. M. How were you received.
S. W. On the angle of the square at my naked right breast, which was to teach me that the square of virtue should be a rule and guide to my conduct in all my future action with mankind.
W. M. How were you then disposed of?
S. W. I was conducted twice about the altar to the Junior Warden in the South, where the same questions were asked and like answers returned as at the door.
W. M. How did the Junior Warden dispose of you?
S. W. He directed me to pass on to the Senior Warden in the West, where the same questions were asked and like answers returned as before.
W. M. How did the Senior Warden dispose of you?
S. W. He directed me to the Worshipful Master in the East, where the same questions were asked and like answers returned as before.
W. M. How did the Worshipful Master dispose of you?

FELLOW CRAFT, OR SECOND DEGREE.

S. W. He ordered me to be reconducted to the Senior Warden in the West, who taught me to approach to the East, advancing by two upright, regular steps, my feet forming the right angle of an oblong square, my body erect to the Worshipful Master in the East.

W. M. What did the Worshipful Master then do with you?

S. W. He made me a Fellow Craft.

W. M. How?

S. W. In due form.

W. M. What is the due form?

S. W. Kneeling on my naked right knee, my left forming a square, my body erect, my naked right hand resting on the Holy Bible, square and compasses, my left elbow forming a right angle, cupported by the square; in which due form I took the obligation of a Fellow Craft.

W. M. What was the obligation?

S. W. I, A. B., of my own free will and accord, in the presence, etc. *(See page 95.)*

W. M. After taking the obligation, what were you then asked?

S. W. What I most desired.

W. M. Your answer?

S. W. More light in Masonry.

W. M. Did you receive it?

S. W. I did.

W. M. How?

S. W. By order of the Worshipful Master and assistance of the brethren.

W. M. On being brought to light, what did you

FELLOW CRAFT, OR SECOND DEGREE.

first discover more than you had heretofore discovered?

S. W. One point of the compasses bare, the other being hidden; which was to teach me that as yet I had received light in Masonry but partially.

W. M. What did you then discover?

S. W. The Worshipful Master approaching me from the East, under the due guard and sign of a Fellow Craft; who, in token of the continuance of his brotherly love and favor, presented me with his right hand, and with it the pass, token of the pass, grip and word of a Fellow Craft, and bade me arise and salute the Wardens as such.

W. M. After saluting the Wardens, what did you then discover?

S. W. The Worshipful Master, who ordered me to the Senior Warden, who taught me how to wear my apron as a Fellow Craft.

W. M. After being taught how to wear your apron as a Fellow Craft, how were you then disposed of?

S. W. I was conducted to the right hand of the Worshipful Master in the East, who presented me with the working tools of a Fellow Craft and taught me their uses.

W. M. What are the working tools of a Fellow Craft?

S. W. The plumb, square and level.

W. M. What are their uses?

S. W. The plumb is an instrument, etc. *(See page 99)* —— from whose bourne no traveler returns.

W. M. How were you then disposed of?

FELLOW CRAFT, OR SECOND DEGREE.

S. W. I was ordered to be reconducted to the place from whence I came, there be reinvested of what I had been divested, and informed that agreeable to an ancient custom in all regular and well-governed Lodge of Fellow Crafts, it was then necessary that I should make a regular ascent up a flight of winding stairs, consisting of three, five and seven steps, into a place representing the middle chamber of King Solomon's Temple, there to receive further instruction relative to the wages of a Fellow Craft, which are corn, wine and oil, emblematical of peace, unity and plenty.

SECTION II.

W. M. How many kinds of Masonry are there?

S. W. Two—operative and speculative.

W. M. What is meant by operative Masonry?

S. W. By operative Masonry we allude to a proper application of the useful rules of, etc. *(See page 100)* ——— and beneficent purposes.

W. M. What is meant by speculative Masonry?

S. W. By speculative Masonry we learn to subdue the passions, act upon the square, keep, etc. *(See page 101)* ——— of his Divine Creator.

W. M. Have you ever worked as a Mason?

S. W. I have as a speculative Mason only, but our ancient brethren worked both in operative and speculative Masonry.

W. M. How long did they work before they received wages?

S. W. Six days.

W. M. Did they not work on the seventh?

FELLOW CRAFT, OR SECOND DEGREE.

S. W. They did not.

W. M. Why not?

S. W. Because in six days God created the heavens and the earth, and rested upon the seventh day; the seventh, therefore, our ancient brethren created as a day of rest from their labors, thereby enjoying frequent opportunities to contemplate the glorious works of the creation and to adore their great Creator.

W. M. Where were you received and recorded as a Fellow Craft?

S. W. In a place representing the middle chamber of King Solomon's Temple.

W. M. Did you observe anything that particularly attracted your attention on your passage there?

S. W. I did.

W. M. What?

S. W. Two great pillars; one on the right hand, the other on the left.

W. M. What is the one on the left hand called?

S. W. Boaz.

W. M. What does that denote?

S. W. Strength.

W. M. What is the one on the right hand called?

S. W. Jachin.

W. M. What does that denote?

S. W. Establishment.

W. M. To what do they collectively allude?

S. W. To the promise of God to David, that he would establish his kingdom in strength.

W. M. Where were these pillars cast?

S. W. In the clay grounds on the banks of Jor-

FELLOW CRAFT, OR SECOND DEGREE.

dan, between Succoth and Zarthan, where all the vessels of King Solomon's Temple were cast by Hiram Abiff.

W. M. Who was Hiram Abiff?
S. W. The widow's son of the tribe of Naphtali.
W. M. Were they cast hollow or solid?
S. W. Hollow.
W. M. Why so?
S. W. The better to serve as a safe deposit for the archives of Masonry against all conflagrations and inundations.
W. M. How high were they?
S. W. Thirty-five cubits each.
W. M. How were they adorned?
S. W. With chapiters of five cubits, making in all forty cubits in height.
W. M. How were these adorned?
S. W. With lily-work, network and pomegranates.
W. M. What do they denote?
S. W. Peace, unity and plenty.
W. M. Why so?
S. W. The lily by its purity, and the retired situation in which it grows, denotes peace; the network, by the intimate connection of its parts, denotes unity; the pomegranates, by the exuberance of their seed, denote plenty.
W. M. How were they further adorned? What are their uses? What do they further denote?
S. W. With globes on their tops, representing the terrestrial and celestial spheres. These globes are two artificial, etc. *(See page 102)* by which society has been so much benefited. They also denote the universality of the earth.

FELLOW CRAFT, OR SECOND DEGREE.

W. M. After passing the porch, where did you next arrive?

S. W. At a flight of winding stairs, consisting of three, five and seven steps.

W. M. To what does the number three allude?

S. W. To the first three degrees of Masonry, and also to the three principal officers of the Lodge.

W. M. To what does the number five allude

S. W. To the five orders in Architecture.

W. M. What is meant by Order in Architecture?

S. W. By Order in Architecture is meant a system of all the members, proportions and ornaments of columns and pilasters. Or it is a regular arrangement of the projecting parts of a building, which, united with those of a column, form a beautiful, perfect and complete work.

W. M. How are these orders classed?

S. Wi. The five orders are thus classed: The Tuscan, Doric, Ionic, Corinthian and Composite. The Tuscan is the most simple, etc. *(See page 104)*——— is generally found in buildings where strength, elegance and beauty are displayed.

W. M. Which of these are most revered by Masons?

S. W. The ancient and original orders.

W. M. What are they?

S. W. They are the Doric, Ionic and Corinthian, which were invented by the Greeks. To these the Romans have added, etc. *(see page 106)*———for what is great, judicious and distinct in Architecture.

W. M. To what does the number five further allude?

FELLOW CRAFT, OR SECOND DEGREE.

S. W. To the five senses of human nature: Hearing, seeing, feeling, smelling and tasting. Hearing is that sense, etc. *(See page 106)*———indebted for creation, preservation and every blessing we enjoy.

W. M. Which of these are most revered by Masons?

S. W. The first three: Hearing, seeing and feeling.

W. M. Why so?

S. W. Because by the sense of hearing we distinguish the word, by that of seeing we perceive the sign, and by that of feeling we receive the grip, whereby one Mason may know another in the dark as well as in the light.

W. M. To what does the number seven allude?

S. W. To the seven liberal arts and sciences: Grammar, rhetoric, logic, arithmetic, geometry, music and astronomy. Grammar teaches the proper arrangement, etc. *(See page 109)*———whose relation or affinity to another is already known or discovered. Music teaches the art of forming, etc. *(See page 111)*———and, through the whole creation, trace the glorious Author by His works.

W. M. Which of these is mose revered by Masons?

S. W. Geometry, or the fifth science.

W. M. What does geometry treat of?

S. W. Geometry treats of the powers and properties of magnitudes in general, etc. *(See page 110)* ———namely, length, breadth and thickness.

W. M. What are its advantages?

S. W. By this science the architect is enabled to

FELLOW CRAFT, OR SECOND DEGREE.

construct his plans and execute, etc. *(See page 111)* ———the foundation of architecture and the root of the mathematics.

W. M. After passing the stairs, where did you next arrive?

S. W. At the outer door of the middle chamber, which I found guarded by the Junior Warden, who demanded of me the pass and token of the pass of a Fellow Craft.

W. M. Give me the pass.

S. W. *The pass is given.*

W. M. What does that denote?

S. W. Plenty.

W. M. How is it represented?

S. W. By an ear of corn hanging near a waterford.

W. M. From whence originated this word?

S. W. In consequence of a quarrel between Jephtha, Judge of Israel, and the Ephraimites. The Ephraimites having, etc. *(See page 112)*———into all regular and well-governed Lodges of Fellow Crafts.

W. M. After passing the outer door, where did you next arrive?

S. W. At the inner door of the middle chamber, which I found guarded by the Senior Warden, who demanded of me the grip and word of a Fellow Craft.

W. M. Give me the grip.

The Senior Warden gives the grip, and then follow five questions and answers which relate only to the details of the grip, etc.

FELLOW CRAFT, OR SECOND DEGREE.

W. M. After passing the inner door, where did you next arrive?

S. W. Within the middle chamber, where I found the Worshipful Master, who was pleased to explain to me the various objects which had attracted my attention on my passage there, and directed my attention to an emblem or letter G, universally displayed over the Master's chair. He informed me that it was the initial of geometry.

W. M. What explanation did the Worshipful Master give you of geometry?

S. W. Geometry, the first and nblest of sciences, is the basis on which, etc. *(See page 114)*——— transmitted unimpaired the excellent tenets of our institution.

W. M. What further explanation did the Worshipful Master give you of the letter G?

S. W. He informed me that it alluded to the sacred name of Deity, before whom we should all, from the youngest Entered Apprentice in the Northeast corner to the Worshipful Master who presides in the East, with reverence most humbly bow.

CLOSING A LODGE OF FELLOW CRAFTS.

At the conclusion of the lecture, the Lodge of Fellow Crafts is closed in the following manner:

The Master calls up the Deacons by one rap.

W. M. to J. D. Brother Junior Deacon what is the last great care of Masons when in Lodge assembled?

J. D. To see that the Lodge is duly tyled, Worshipful Master.

FELLOW CRAFT, OR SECOND DEGREE.

W. M. to J. D. Perform that duty; inform the Tyler that I am about to close this Lodge of Fellow Crafts.

The Junior Deacon obeys the order, and says:

J. D. The Lodge is duly tyled, Worshipful Master.

W. M. to J. D. How are we tyled, brother Junior Deacon?

J. D. By a brother Master Mason without the door, armed with the proper instrument of his office.

W. M. What are his dutes there?

J. D. To keep off all cowans and eavesdroppers, and to see that none pass or repass but such as are duly qualified and have permission from the Worshipful Master.

The Master seats the Deacons by one rap.

W. M. to S. W. Brother Senior Warden, are you a Fellow Craft?

S. W. I am; try me.

W. M. How will you be tried?

S. W. By the square.

W. M. Why by the square?

S. W. Because it is one of the working tools of my profession.

W. M. What is a square?

S. W. An angle of ninety degrees, or the fourth part of a circle.

W. M. Where were you made a Fellow Craft?

S. W. In a just and lawfully constituted Lodge of Fellow Crafts.

W. M. How many anciently composed a Lodge of Fellow Crafts?

FELLOW CRAFT, OR SECOND DEGREE.

S. W. Five or more.

W. M. When composed of only five, who were they?

S. W. The Worshipful Master, Senior Warden, Junior Warden, Senior Deacon and Junior Deacon.

W. M. What is the Junior Deacon's place in the Lodge?

S. W. At the right of the Senior Warden in the West.

W. M. to J. D. What are your duties there, brother Junior Deacon?

J. D. To carry messages from the Senior Warden in the West to the Junior aWrden in the South, and elsewhere about the Lodge as he may direct, and to see that the Lodge is duly tyled.

W. M. What is the Senior Deacon's place in the Lodge?

J. D. On the right of the Worshipful Master in the East.

W. M. to S. D. What are your duties there, brother Senior Deacon?

S. D. To carry orders from the Worshipful Master in the East to the Senior Warden in the West, and elsewhere about the Lodge as he may direct; to welcome and accommodate visiting brthren; to receive and conduct candidates.

W. M. What is the Junior Warden's place in the Lodge?

S. D. In the South.

W. M. to J. W. Why are you in the South, brother Junior Warden. What are your duties there?

FELLOW CRAFT, OR SECOND DEGREE.

J. W. As the Sun in the South at its meridian height is the glory and beauty of the day, so stands the Junior Warden in the South, the better to observe the time; to call the craft from labor to refreshment; to superintend them during the hours thereof, and see that they do not convert the purposes of refreshment into intemperance and excess; to call them on again in due season, that the Worshipful Master may have pleasure and the craft profit thereby.

W. M. What is the Senior Warden's station in the Lodge?

J. W. In the West.

W. M. to S. W. Why are you in the West, brother Senior Warden? What are your duties there?

S. W. As the Sun is in the West at the close of the day, so is the Senior Warden in the West to assist the Worshipful Master in opening and closing his Lodge; to pay the craft their wages, if any be due, and see that none go away dissatisfied, harmony being the strength and support of all societies, more especially of ours.

W. M. What is the Worshipful Master's station in the Lodge?

S. W. In the East.

W. M. Why is he in the East, brother Senior Warden? What are his duties there?

S. W. As the Sun rises in the East to open and govern the day, so rises the Worshipful Master in the East to open and govern his Lodge; to set the craft to work, and give them good and wholesome instruction for their labors.

FELLOW CRAFT, OR SECOND DEGREE.

The Master now calls up the Lodge by three raps, himself rising last.

W. M. to S. W. Brother Senior Warden, it is my will and pleasure that this Lodge of Fellow Crafts be now closed. Communicate this order to the Junior Warden in the South, and he to the craft for their government.

S. W. to J. W. It is the will and pleasure of the Worshipful Master in the East that this Lodge of Fellow Crafts be now closed. Communicate this order to the craft for their government.

J. W. to Lodge. Brethren, it is the will and pleasure of the Worshipful Master in the East, communicated to me by the Senior Warden in the West, that this Lodge of Fellow Crafts be now closed; take notice and govern yourselves accordingly.—Look to the East!

The signs are now given and the raps passed twice about the stations.

W. M. to Lodge. In the name of God and the Holy Saints John I declare this Lodge of Fellow Crafts closed in form. Brother Junior Deacon, inform the Tyler.

The Master now requests all those present who are not Master Masons to retire. The Junior Deacon communicates the Master's order to the Tyler. The Senior Deacon closes the three Great Lights.

The Master seats the Deacons by one rap, and the Lodge is called up to the third degree as follows:

W. M. to S. W. Brother Senior Warden, proceed to satisfy yourself that all present are Master Masons.

FELLOW CRAFT, OR SECOND DEGREE.

When this order is obeyed, the Senior Warden reports to the Master:

S. W. to M. W. All present are Master Masons.

The Master calls up the Senior and Junior Deacon by one rap.

W. M. to J. D. Brother Junior Deacon, what is the first great care of Masons when in Lodge assembled?

J. D. to W. M. To see that the Lodge is duly tyled, Worshipful Master.

W. M. Perform that duty, and inform the Tyler that we are about to resum labor as Master Masons.

The Junior Deacon obeys this oredr, and reports to the Woshipful Master as follows:

J. D. The Lodge is duly tyled, Worshipful Master.

W. M. How are we tyled, brother Junior Deacon?

J. D. By a brother Master Mason without the door, armed with the proper instrument of his office.

W. M. What are his duties there?

J. D. To keep off all cowans and eavesdroppers, and see hat none pass or repass but such as are duly qualified and have permission from the Worshipful Master.

The Master gives one rap, which seats the Deacons.

W. M. to J. W. Brother Junior Warden, how goes the hour?

J. W. to W. M. One hour past high twelve. Worshipful Master.

W. M. It being one hour past high twelve, you will call the craft from refreshment to labor on the third degree.

FELLOW CRAFT, OR SECOND DEGREE.

The Junior Warden calls up the Lodge by three raps.

J. W. to Lodge. Brethren, it is the will and pleasure of the Worshipful Master in the East that this Lodge be called from refreshment to labor on the third degree; take notice and govern yourselves accordingly.—Look to the East!

The signs are given and the raps passed about the stations three times, as at opening. The Master then continues:

W. M. to Lodge. I declare this Lodge at labor on the third degree. Brother Junior Deacon, inform the Tyler. Brother Senior Deacon, arrange the three Great Lights.

The Junior Deacon reports, and the Great Lights are displayed to correspond with the degree.

W. M. to S. W. Brother Senior Warden, have you anything in the West to come before this Lodge of Master Masons?

S. W. Nothing n the West, Worshipful Master.

W. M. to J. W. Anything in the South, brother Junior Warden?

J. W. Nothing in the South, Worshipful Master.

W. M. to Sec. Brother Secretary, have you anything on your table?

Sec. Nothing, Worshipful Master.

W. M. to J. D. Brother Junior Deacon, what is the last great care of Masons when in Lodge assembled?

J. D. To see that the Lodge is duly tyled, Worshipful Master.

W. M. Perform that duty, and inform the Tyler

FELLOW CRAFT, OR SECOND DEGREE.

that I am about to close this Lodge of Master Masons.

The Junior Deacon opens the door and communicates the Master's order, and reports:

J. D. to W. M. The Lodge is duly tyled, Worshipful Master.

W. M. How are we tyled, brother Junior Deacon?

J. D. By a brother Master Mason without the door, armed with the proper instrument of his office.

W. M. What are his duties there?

J. D. To keep off all cowans and eavesdroppers, and to see that none pass or repass but such as are duly qualified and have permission from the Worshipful Master.

The Worshipful Master now seats the Deacons by one rap.

W. M. to S. W. Are you a Master Mason?

S. W. I am.

W. M. What induced you to become a Master Mason?

S. W. In order that I might receive Masters' wages, and better to be enabled to support myself and family, and contribute to the relief of poor, distressed Master Masons, their widows and orphans.

W. M. Where were you made a Master Mason?

S. W. In a just and lawfully constituted Lodge of Master Masons.

W. M. How many anciently composed a Lodge of Master Masons?

S. W. Three or more.

W. M. When composed of only three, who were they?

FELLOW CRAFT, OR SECOND DEGREE.

S. W. The Worshipful Master, Senior Warden and Junior Warden.

W. M. What is the Junior Warden's station in the Lodge?

S. . In the South.

W. M. to J. W. Why are you in the South, brother Junior Warden? What are your duties there?

J. W. to W. M. As the Sun in the South at its meridian height is the glory and beauty of the day, so stands the Junior Warden in the South, the better to observe the time; to call the craft from labor to refreshment; to superintend them during the hours thereof, and see that they do not convert the purposes of refreshment into intemperance and excess; to call them on again in due season, that the Worshipful Master may have pleasure and the craft profit thereby.

W. M. to J. W. What is the Senior Warden's station in the Lodge?

J. W. In the West.

W. M. to S. Why are you in the West, brother Senior Warden? What are your duties there?

S. W. to W. M. As the Sun is in the West at the close of the day, so is the Senior Warden in the West to assist the Worshipful Master in opening and closing his Lodge; to pay the craft their wages, if any be due, and see that none go away dissatisfied, harmony being the strength and support of all societies, more especially of ours.

W. M. to S. W. What is the Worshipful Master's station in the Lodge?

S. W. to W. M. In the East.

FELLOW CRAFT, OR SECOND DEGREE.

W. M. to S. W. Why is he in the East, brother Senior Warden? What are his duties there?

S. W. to W. M. As the sun rises in the East to open and govern the day, so rises the Worshipful Master in the East to open and govern his Lodge; to set the craft to work, and give them good and wholesome instruction for their labors.

The Master calls up the Lodge by three raps.

W. M. to S. W. Brother Senior Warden, it is my will and pleasure that —— Lodge number —— be now closed. Communicate this order to the Junior Warden in the South, and he to the craft for their government.

S. W. to J. W. Brother Junior Warden, it is the will and pleasure of the Worshipful Master in the East that —— Lodge number —— be now closed; communicate this order to the craft for their government.

J. W. to Lodge. Brethren, it is the will and pleasure of the Worshipful Master in the East, communicated to me by the Senior Warden in the West, that —— Lodge number —— be now closed; take notice and govern. yourselves accordingly.— Look to the East!

The signs are now given, the raps passed about the stations three times, and the usual prayer is offered. When this is done, the Master asks the following questions:

W. M. to S. W. Brother Senior Warden, how do Masons meet?

S. W. Upon the level, Worshipful Master.

W. M. Brother Junior Warden, how do Masons act?

FELLOW CRAFT, OR SECOND DEGREE.

J. W. Upon the plumb, Worshipful Master.

W. M. to Lodge. And they part upon the square. So may we meet, act and part. May the blessings of heaven rest upon us and all regular Masons! May brotherly love prevail, and every moral and social virtue cement us! In the name of God and the Holy Saints John I declare this Lodge closed in form. Brother Junior Deacon, inform the Tyler.

The Master gives three raps and the craft are dismissed. The Junior Deacon gives three raps at the door, which are answered by the Tyler, and as soon as the Master's orders are communicated to him, the door is thrown open for the brethren to depart.

Meanwhile the Senior Deacon closes the Great Lights, and places them on the Secretary's table, who secures them in the proper place. The Lesser Lights are removed, and the Wardens reverse their columns, down in the West, erect in the South.

MASTER MASON, OR THIRD DEGREE.

When the regular time for opening has arrived, the Master repairs to his station and calls the Lodge to order with one rap of his gavel. The door is shut; the brethren clothe themselves and take their seats; the officers put on their jewels; the Wardens dispose of their columns, down in the West, erect in the South; the Deacons take their rods; the Secretary lays his books and papers and the three Great Lights upon his table, and in a few moments the Lodge is silent and in order for the opening. The Master then proceeds as follows:

W. M. to S. W. Brother Senior Warden, proceed to satisfy yourself that all present are Master Masons.

The Senior Warden rises and makes a personal observation of every. one that is present. He then requests the Senior and Junior Deacons to give to him, in a whisper, the pass of a Master Mason, and to demand it, under the same conditions, from each person present except the Worshipful Master, Senior Warden and Junior Warden. After this is done, the Junior Deacon communicates the pass to the Senior Deacon and he to the Worshipful Master.

W. M. to S. W. The pass is ———.

S. W. to M. W. All present are Master Masons, Worshipful Master.

When any one addresses the Master during any Masonic ceremony, he must rise and salute.

MASTER MASON, OR THIRD DEGREE.

The Worshipful Master calls up the Senior Deacon and Junior Deacon by one rap.

W. M. to J. D. Brother Junior Deacon, what is the first great care of Masons when in Lodge assembled?

J. D. to W. M. To see that the Lodge is duly tyled, Worshipful Master.

W. M. to J. D. Perform that duty; inform the Tyler that I am about to open a Lodge of Master Masons, and direct him to tyle accordingly.

The Junior Deacon opens the door without knocking, and satisfies himself that the Tyler is at his post, he then communicates to him the Master's orders and shuts the door. The Tyler then locks the door on the outside.

J. D. to W. M. The Lodge is duly tyled, Worshipful Master.

W. M. to J. D. How are we tyled, brother Junior Deacon?

J. D. to W. M. By a brother Master Mason without the door, armed with the proper instrument of his office.

W. M. to J. D. What are his duties there?

J. D. to W. M. To keep off all cowans and eavesdroppers, and to see that none pass or repass but such as are duly qualified and have permission from the Worshipful Master.

The Master then seats the Senior and Junior Deacons with one rap.

W. M. to S. W. Are you a Master Mason?

S. W. I am.

W. M. What induced you to become a Master Mason?

MASTER MASON, OR THIRD DEGREE.

S. W. In order that I might receive Masters' wages, and be thereby better enabled to support myself and family, and contribute to the relief of poor, distressed Master Masons, their widows and orphans.

W. M. to S. W. Where were you made a Master Mason?

S. W. to W. M. In a just and lawfully constituted Lodge of Master Masons.

After having rehearsed as much of the lecture as he deems necessary, the Master proceeds as follows:

W. M. to S. W. How many anciently composed a Lodge of Master Masons?

S. W. to W. M. Three or more.

W. M. to S. W. When composed of only three, who were they?

S. W. to W. M. The Worshipful Master, Senior Warden and Junior Warden.

W. M. to S. W. What is the Junior Warden's station in the Lodge?

S. W. to W. M. In the South.

W. M. Why are you in the South, brother Junior Warden? What are your duties there?

J. W. As the Sun in the South at its Meridian height is the glory and beauty of the day, so stands the Junior Warden in the South, the better to observe the time; to call the craft from labor to refreshment; to superintend them during the hours thereof, and see that they do not convert the purposes of refreshment into intemperance and excess; to call them on again in due season, that the Worshipful Master may have pleasure and the craft profit thereby.

MASTER MASON, OR THIRD DEGREE.

W. M. What is the Senior Warden's station in the Lodge?

J. W. In the West.

W. M. Why are you in the West, brother Senior Warden? What are your duties there?

S. W. As the Sun is in the West at the close of the day, so is the Senior Warden in the West to assist the Worshipful Master in opening and closing his Lodge; to pay the craft their wages, if any be due, and see that none go away dissatisfied, harmony being the strength and support of all societies, more especially of ours.

W. M. What is the Worshipful Master's station in the Lodge?

S. W. In the East.

W. M. Why is he in the East, brother Senior Warden? What are his duties there?

S. W. As the sun rises in the East to open and govern the day, so rises the Worshipful Master in the East to open and govern his Lodge; to set the craft to work, and give them good and wholesome instruction for their labors.

This closes the opening lecture. The Master gives three raps, which call up the Lodge, he rising last.

W. M. Brother Senior Warden, it is my will and pleasure that ⎯⎯ Lodge number ⎯⎯ be now opened on the third degree of Masonry, for the dispatch of such business as may regularly come before it, under the usual Masonic restrictions. Communicate this order to the Junior Warden in the South and he to the craft for their government.

S. W. to J. W. *(turning to that officer in the*

MASTER MASON, OR THIRD DEGREE.

South.) Brother Junior Warden, it is the will and pleasure of the Worshipful Master in the East that ——— Lodge number ——— be now opened on the third degree of Masonry, for the dispatch of such business as may regularly come before it, under the usual Masonic restrictons. Communicate this order to the craft for their government.

J. W. to Lodge. Brethren, it is the will and pleasure of the Worshipful Master in the East, communicated to me by the Senior Warden in the West, that ——— Lodge number ——— be now opened on the third degree of Masonry, for the dispatch of such business as may regularly come before it, under the usual Masonic restrictions. Take notice and govern yourselves accordingly.—Look to the East!

W. M. to Lodge. Brethren, together, and the signs.

The craft all face towards the Worshipful Master, who makes, slowly and distinctly, the signs of an Entered Apprentice, Fellow Craft and Master Mason, successively, which are imitated simultaneously by the craft.

After the signs have been made the Junior Warden gives one rap with his gavel, followed by the Senior Warden in the West and by the Master in the East. These raps are passed thrice about the stations.

The Master now takes off his hat and says: "Let us pry."

The prayer is offered by the Master or Chaplain. After prayer the Master announces to the Lodge:

W. M. In the name of God and the Holy Saints

MASTER MASON, OR THIRD DEGREE.

John, I declare ―――― Lodge number ―――― opened in form on the third degree. Brother Junior Deacon, inform the Tyler.

The Master seats the craft by one rap. The Junior Deacon goes to the door and knocks thrice upon it, on which it is opened by the Tyler, to whom the Junior Deacon announces that the Lodge is opened in the third degree. He then shuts the door, which is locked on the outside by the Tyler.

J. D. to W. M. The duty is performed, Worshipful Master.

The Master seats the Junior Deacon by one rap. While this in progress, the Senior Deacon takes the three Great Lights from the Secretary's table and arranges them duly upon the altar, the Bible laying open at Eccesiastes xii, and both points of the compasses above the square.

The Lesser Lights are placed in their proper position, two at the North-east and North-west corners of the altar, and the third between them, a little further Northward. The Wardens reverse their columns, erect in the West, down in the South.

After the ceremonies of opening are concluded, the Master requests the Secretary to read the minutes of their last regular communication. This being done, the Master asks as follows:

W. M. to S. W. Brother Senior Warden, have you any alterations to propose?

If the Senior Warden has any remarks to make he now does so, first making the sign of a Master Mason. If he has nothing to offer by way of amendment, he says:

MASTER MASON, OR THIRD DEGREE.

S. W. to W. M. *(making the sign of a Master Mason.)* I have none, Worshipful Master.

W. M. to J. W. Have you any, brother Junior Warden?

J. W. to W. M. *(making the sign).* None, Worshipful Master.

W. M. to Lodge. Has any brother around the Lodge any alterations to propose?

If none are offered the Master puts the question of the adoption of the minutes, etc., and then follows the other regular business of the Lodge, viz:

2. Reading and referreing petitions.
3. Reports of Committees.
4. Balloting for Candidates.
5. Conferring Degrees.
6. Unfinished business.
7. Disposing of such other business as may lawfully come before the Lodge.

When the Master announces the fifth order of business *(conferring degrees)*, he proceeds as follows:

W. M. to J. D. Brother Junior Deacon, you will ascertain whether there are any candidates in waiting, and if so, who, and for what degree.

The Junior Deacon proceeds to the preparation room, and having ascertained that a candidate is there, reports as follows:

J. D. to W. M. Worshipful Master, brother A. B. is in waiting for the third degree.

The seventh and last order of business includes the work of initiation, passing and raising, and when all the other business of the Lodge has been transacted, the Master proceeds as follows:

MASTER MASON, OR THIRD DEGREE.

W. M. Brother Stewards, you will repair to the preparation room, where you will find brother A. B. in waiting, whom you will duly prepare for raising to the sublime degree of Master Mason.

CEREMONIES OF RAISING.

The Stewards step to the altar, make the proper sign, and leaving the altar on their right, proceed to the preparation room, where they question the candidate in the customary manner, and prepare him in due form for the ceremonies of raising, his apron being worn as a Fellow Craft.

They then require him to make three distinct knocks on the door, on hearing which the Senior Deacon rises and says:

S. D. Worshipful Master, there is an alarm at the door of the preparation room.

W. M. to S. D. Attend to the alarm.

The Senior Deacon, leaving the altar on his right, proceeds to the door of the preparation room and gives three knocks upon it. The door is then opened by the Stewards just sufficient to admit of conversation.

S. D. Who comes here?

Steward. A brother who has been regularly initiated as an Entered Apprentice, passed to the degree of a Fellow Craft, and now wishes to receive further light in Masonry by being raised to the sublime degree of a Master Mason.

S. D. to Candidate. Is it of your own free will and accord?

Candidate. It is.

MASTER MASON, OR THIRD DEGREE.

S. D. to Steward. Is he duly and truly prepared?
Steward. He is.
S. D. Is he worthy and well qualified?
Steward. He is.
S. D. Has he made a suitable proficiency in the preceding degrees?
Steward. He has.
S. D. By what further right or benefit does he expect to gain admission?
Steward. By the benefit of the pass.
S. D. Has he the pass?
Steward. He has it not; I have it for him.
S. D. Give me the pass.

The pass is given by the Steward to the Senior Deacon in a low whisper.

S. D. Let him wait with patience until the Worshipful Master is informed of his request, and his answer returned.

The Senior Deacon closes the door, proceeds to the altar, salutes the Master, and gives three knocks on the floor with his rod.

W. M. Who comes there?
S. D. A brother who has been regularly initiated as an Entered Appretice, passed to the degree of a Fellow Craft, and now wishes to receive further light in Masonry by being raised to the sublime degree of a Master Mason.
W. M. Is it of his own free will and accord.
S. D. It is.
W. M. Is he duly and truly prepared?
S. D. He is.
W. M. Is he worthy and well qualified?

MASTER MASON, OR THIRD DEGREE.

S. D. He is.

W. M. Has he made suitable proficiency in the preceding degrees?

S. D. He has.

W. M. Since he comes endowed with all these essential qualifications, it is my will and pleasure that he enter this Lodge of Master Masons, and that you receive him in due and ancient form.

The Senior Deacon returns to the door of the preparation room, opens it wide, and says to the Stewards:

S. D. It is the will and pleasure of the Worshipful Master that he enter this Lodge of Master Masons.

The Stewards, one on each side of the candidate, conduct him into the Lodge. They then close the door behind them and take their seats. The Senior Deacon now takes charge of the candidate, and addresses him as follows:

S. D. to Candidate. My brother, it is the will and pleasure of the Worshipful Master that I receive you into this Lodge of Master Masons in due and ancient form. You are received upon both points of the compasses, extending from your naked right to left breasts; which is to signify that as the vital parts of man are contained within the breasts, so the most useful tenets of our institution are contained within the two points of the compasses, which are friendship, morality and brotherly love.

The Senior Deacon takes the candidate's left hand in his own right, and conducts him, with slow and measured steps, nearly to the N. E. corner of the Lodge; when they have reached that point, they

MASTER MASON, OR THIRD DEGREE.

turn at right angles and proceed nearly to the S. E. corner; thence to the S. W. corner; thence to the N .W. corner, and so on, moving in direct lines, and making three complete circuits about the Lodge. As they pass the first time by the stations of the Senior Warden, Junior Warden and Master, each of these officers gives one rap. The second passage is greeted by each officer by two raps; and the third by three raps; and as soon as the Junior Warden gives his first rap, the Master commences to read the 12th chap. of Ecclesiastes, and times the reading so as to conclude at the some time the circuits are finished. The Senior Deacon then conducts the candidate in front of, and one pace distant from, the Junior Warden's station in the South, where he gives three knocks on the floor with his rod.

J. W. Who comes there?

S. D. A brother who has been regularly initiated as an Entered Apprentice, passed to the degree of a Fellow Craft, and now wishes to receive further light in Masonry by being raised to the sublime degree of a Master Mason.

J. W. to Candidate. Is it of your own free will and accord?

Candidate. It is.

J. W. Is he duly and truly prepared?

S. D. He is.

J. W. Is he worthy and well qualified?

S. D. He is.

J. W. Has he made suitable proficiency in the preceding degrees?

S. D. He has.

MASTER MASON, OR THIRD DEGREE.

J. W. By what further right or benefit does he expect to gain admission?

S. D. By the benefit of the pass.

J. W. Has he the pass?

S. D. He has it not; I have it for him.

J. W. Advance and give it.

The Senior Deacon advances and gives the pass.

J. W. Conduct the candidate to the Senior Warden in the West for further examination.

The Senior Deacon and candidate pass on to the front of the Senior Warden's station, where the Senior Deacon gives three knocks with his rod, and the same questions and answers are given and received as at the Junior Warden's station. The Senior Deacon gives the Senior Warden the pass.

The Senior Warden then orders them to the Master's station for final examination and instruction, where the same ceremony is repeated, and at the conclusion the Master says:

W. M. From whence come you and whither are you traveling?

S. D. From the West, and traveling to the East.

W. M. Of what are you in pursuit?

S. D. That which is lost, which, by my endeavors and your assistance, I am in hopes to find.

W. M. To what do you refer?

S. D. To the secrets of a Master Mason.

W. M. Your pursuit is truly laudable. *(To Candidate.)* You will be reconducted to the Senior Warden in the West, who will teach you how to approach to the East, advancing by three upright, regular steps, your feet forming the right angle of a

MASTER MASON, OR THIRD DEGREE.

perfect square, your body erect to the Worshipful Master in the East.

The Senior Deacon conducts the candidate to the Senior Warden in the West, leaving the altar on his right as he passes it.

S. D. to S. W. Brother Senior Warden, it is the will and pleasure of the Worshipful Master in the East that this brother be taught to approach to the East, advancing by three upright, regular steps, his feet forming the right angle of a perfect square, his body erect to the Worshipful Master in the East.

S. W. to S. D. You will see that the Worshipful Master's orders are obeyed.

S. D. to. Candidate. You will face to the East. Step off with your left foot as an Entered Apprentice; now take another step with your right foot as a Fellow Craft, and now take another step with your left foot and bring the heel of the right foot to the heel of the left foot, the feet forming the right angle of a perfect square, your body erect to the Worshipful Master in the East. *(To W. M.)* Your orders have been obeyed, Worshipful Master.

While the candidate is in this position, the Master addresses him from the chair as follows:

W. M. to Candidate. My brother, you are now advancing to the last and highest grade of ancient craft Masonry, the sublime degree of a Master Mason. The obligations of this degree are numerous and extremely weighty. Were it not that your trust is in God, and you are taught to apply to Him for strength and wisdom, you might well shrink from assuming them. They cannot be repudiated or

MASTER MASON, OR THIRD DEGREE.

laid aside. Yet, as before, I am free to inform you that these new obligations, like those you have heretofore taken, contain nothing which can conflict with your duty to God, your country your neighbor or yourself. With this renewed pledge on my part, as Master of the Lodge, I ask you, are you willing to take such an obligation, as all Masons have done before you?

The candidate assenting, the Master proceeds:

W. M. to S. D. Place the candidate in due form to be made a Master Mason.

S. D. to Candidate. Advance! Kneel upon your naked knees; your body erect; your naked hands resting on the Holy Bible, square and compasses.

At each direction, the Senior Deacon places the candidate in position accordingly.

S. D. to W. M. The candidate is in due form, Worshipful Master.

The Master calls up the Lodge by three raps, himself rising last. He then uncovers his head, and advancing to the altar, he places his right hand on the Holy Bible.

W. M. to Candidate. You will repeat your name, and say after me:

I, A. B., of my own free will and accord, in the presence of Almighty God and this worshipful Lodge, erected to him and dedicated to the Holy Saints John, de hereby and hereon most solemnly and sincerely promise and swear as I have heretofore done, but with these additions:

That I will not communicate the secrets of a Master Mason to a Fellow Craft, nor those of a Fellow

MASTER MASON, OR THIRD DEGREE.

Craft to an Entered Apprentice, nor those of an Entered Apprentice to the rest of the world, neither these nor any of them to any person or persons whatsoever, except it be a true and lawful brother Mason, or with the body of a just and lawfully constituted Lodge of Masons, nor unto him or them until by strict trial, due examination, or lawful information, I shall have found him or them as lawfully entitled to them as I am myself.

I furtherore promise and swear that I will stand to and abide by all the laws, rules and regulations of a Master Masons' Lodge, so far as the same come to my knowledge.

I furthermore promise and swear that I will stand swer and obey all due signs and summonses sent me from a Lodge of Master Masons, or handed me by a brother of this degree, if within the length of my cable-tow.

I furthermore promise and swear that I will help, aid and assist all poor, distressed brother Master Masons, their widows and orphans, they applying to me as such, and I deeming them worthy.

I furthermore promise and swear that I will keep the secrets of a brother Master Mason, when communicated to me as such, murder and treason exeopted, and they left to my own choice.

I furthermore promise and swear that I will not be present at, nor give my consent to the making of woman a Mason, an old man in dotage, a young man in nonage, an atheist, an irreligious libertine, a madman or a fool, knowing them to be such.

I furthermore promise and swear that I will not

MASTER MASON, OR THIRD DEGREE.

visit a clandestine Lodge of Masons, nor converse Masonically with a clandestine Mason, or with one who has been suspended or expelled, while under that sentence, knowing him to be such.

I furthemore promise and swear that I will not cheat, wrong or defraud a Lodge of Master Masons, or a brother of this degree, knowing them to be such, but will give them due and timely notice, that they may ward off all approaching danger.

I furthermore promise and swear that I will not violate the chastity of a Master Mason's wife, his mother, sister or daughter, knowing them to be such.

I furthermore promise and swear that I will not give the grand Masonic word in any other manner than that in which I shall receive it, which will be on the five points of fellowship, and then in a low breath.

I furthermore promise and swear that I will not give the grand hailing sign of distress, except it be in case of the most imminent danger, or suffering in the cause of innocence and virtue, or in a just and lawfully constituted Lodge of Master Masons, or in a Lodge for instruction; and when I see or hear it given by a worthy brother in distress, I will fly to the relief of him who gives it, if there be a greater probability of saving his life than losing my own.

All this I most solemnly and sincerely promise and swear, with a firm and steadfast resolution to keep and perform the same, without the least equivocation, mental reservation or self-evasion whatever; binding myself under no less penalty than that of

MASTER MASON, OR THIRD DEGREE.

having my body severed in two, my bowels torn from thence and burned to ashes, and these scattered before the four winds of heaven, that no more remembrance might be had among men or Masons of so vile a wretch as I should be, should I, in the least, knowingly or wittingly violate or transgress this my Master Mason's obligation. So help me God and keep me steadfact.

W. M. to Candidate. In token of your sincerity of purpose in this solemn engagement, you will kiss the Holy Bible, now open before you.

The candidate kisses the Bible.

W. M. to S. D. Brother Senior Deacon, our brother being again bound to us by a covenant which cannot be broken, you will release him from his cable-tow.

The Senior Deacon removes the cable-tow.

W. M. to Candidate. My brother, for by that sacred appellation I again address you, in your present bling condition what do you most desire?

Candidate *(prompted by Senior Deacon)*. Further light in Masonry.

W. M. to Candidate. Further light being your desire, you shall receive it.

W. M. to Lodge. My brethren, you will again stretch forth your hands and assist me in bringing this brother to further light in Masonry.

The brethren all, except the Wardens, come forward and form in two parallel lines from East to West.

W. M. In the beginning God created the heavens and the earth. And the earth was without form

MASTER MASON, OR THIRD DEGREE.

and void; and darkness was upon the face of the deep. And the spirit of God moved upon the face of the waters. And God said, Let there be light, and there was light. In solemn commemoration of that sublime event, I, in like manner, Masonically declare, Let there be light!

At the word "light" all present strike their hands together once, and stamp with their right feet; and at the same instant the Senior Deacon removes the hoodwink.

W. M. And there is light!

W. M. to Candidate. My brother, on being brought to light you discover on the altar before you more than you have hertofore done: both points of the compasses bare, which is to teach us never to lose sight of the Masonic application of this useful and valuable instrument, which teaches friendship, morality and brotherly love.

The Master now retires to the East, and again advances, saying:

W. M. to Candidate. You now discover me approaching you from the East under the due guard and sign of a Master Mason. This, my brother, is the due guard *(gives due guard)* and sign *(makes sign)* of a Master Mason, and alludes to the penalty of your obligation. And upon entering a Lodge of Master Masons, or retiring therefrom, you will always advance to the altar where you now kneel, and salute the Worshipful Master with this due guard and sign. In token of the further continuance of my brotherly love and favor, I again present you with my right hand, and with it the pass and

MASTER MASON, OR THIRD DEGREE.

token of the pass of a Master Mason. Arise, salute the Wardens as a Master Mason.

The Master now returns to his station in the East, and seats himself and the Lodge by one rap. The candidate, conducted by the Senior Deacon, leaves the altar on his right and passes to the Junior Warden's station in the South, where he salutes the Junior Warden with the due guard and sign of a Master Mason. He is then conducted to the Senior Warden in the West whom he salutes in like manner. Finally the candidate is brought to the West of the altar, where he salutes the Master with the same due guard and sign.

W. M. to Candidate. My brother, you will now be reconducted to the Senior Warden in the West, who will teach you how to wear your apron as a Master Mason.

The Senior Deacon conducts the candidate to the Senior Warden, and says:

S. D. to S. W. Brother Senior Warden, it is the will and pleasure of the Worshipful Master in the East that our newly admitted brother be taught how to wear his apron as a Master Mason.

S. W. to S. D. You will see that the order of the Worshipful Master is obeyed.

The Senior Deacon duly invests the candidate, and then conducts him to the right hand of the Master, who thus addresses him:

W. M. to Candidate. I now present you with the working tools of a Master Mason. The working tools of a Master Mason are all the implements of Masonry indiscriminately, but more especially the

MASTER MASON, OR THIRD DEGREE.

trowel. The trowel is an instrument made use of by operative masons to spread the cement which unites a building into one common mass; but we, as Free and Accepted Masons, are taught to make use of it for the more noble and glorious purpose of spreading the cement of brotherly love and affection; that cement which unites us into one sacred band, or society of friends and brothers, among whom no contention should ever exist but that noble contention, or rather emulation, of who best can work or best agree. You will now be reconducted to the place from whence you came, and there be reinvested of what you were divested, and there await my further will and pleasure.

The candidate, after saluting the Master at the altar, is conducted to the preparation room, where the Senior Deacon delivers him to the Stewards. He there resumes his regular clothing, and the Stewards place the jewel of the Junior Warden on his neck. He then returns to the Lodge, salutes the Master, and takes a seat among the other brethren.

The Junior Warden, on yielding up his jewel, vacates his station in the South, and does not resume it until the conferring of the degree is fully completed.

After a short pause, the Master orders the Senior Deacon to conduct the new brother to the East, where he is addressed as follows:

W. M. to Candidate. My brother, you have this evening been obligated by the very solemn and weighty ties of a Master Mason. Having voluntarily assumed this obligation, you were then brought to

MASTER MASON, OR THIRD DEGREE.

light and invested. You have been taught to wear your apron as a Master Mason, and are so wearing it among us at this moment. Even our working tools, the implements of Masonry, have all been explained to you, you have been exhorted to make a proper use of the trowel, the principal working tool of this degree. All this would imply that you are a Master Mason, and qualified to travel and work as such. Nay, more, I observe that you have upon your person a badge of office, the jewel of the Junior Warden, one of the principal officers of the Lodge. This mark of distinction must be highly pleasing to you, and doubtless confirms you in the belief that you are a Master Mason. Is it so?

After a moment's pase, the Senior Deacon answers for the candidate:

S. D. to W. M. He is of that opinion, Worshipful Master.

W. M. to Candidate. My brother, however natural this supposition may be to you, yet it is erroneous. You have not yet atttained to the sublime degree of a Master Mason. You are not yet a Master Mason so far as to enable you to prove yourself one, or to travel or work as one. Nor do I know that ever you will become a Master Mason. You have a way to travel over that is extremely perilous. You will be beset with dangers of many kinds, and may perhaps meet with death, as did once befall an eminent brother of this degree. But your trust is in God and your faith is well founded. Before setting out, therefore, upon so serious an enterprise as this, you will repair to the altar for the purpose of prayer.

MASTER MASON, OR THIRD DEGREE.

Heretofore you had a brother to pray for you; now you must pray for yourself. Go, therefore, my brother, and may the blessing of God accompany you.

The candidate is now conducted to the altar by the Senior Deacon, who hoodwinks him, and directs him to kneel and offer a prayer, mentally or audibly, at the candidate's own discretion.

As he kneels to pray the Master calls up the Lodge by three raps, himself rising last, and when the prayer is ended he seats the Lodge by one rap. The Senior Deacon raises up the candidate and says:

S. D. to Candidate. My brother, heretofore you have represented a candidate in search of more light; now you will represent another character, no less a person than our Grand Master, Hiram Abiff, who was grand architect at the building of King Solomon's Temple. It was the usual custom of this great and good man, at high twelve, when the craft were called from labor to refreshment ,to enter into the sanctum sanctorum or Holy of Holies ,to offer up his adorations to Deity and draw his designs upon his tressel board. This you have done. He then passed out of the south gate to the workmen, as you will now do.

The Senior Deacon takes the candidate by the left hand, conducts him a few steps, and is accosted by a brother representing Jubela.

(This character is usually assumed by the Junior Warden.)

Jubela to Candidate. Grand Master Hiram, I am

MASTER MASON, OR THIRD DEGREE.

glad to meet you thus alone. I have long sought this opportunity. You promised us that when the Temple was completed we should receive the secrets of a Master Mason, whereby we could travel in foreign countries and receive wages as such. Behold! the temple is almost completed, and we have not received what we sought for! At first I did not doubt your veracity, but now I do. I therefore demand of you the secrets of a Master Mason.

S. D. to Ja. Craftsman, this is neither a proper time nor place. Wait until the Temple is completed, and then, if you are found worthy, you shall receive them; otherwise you cannot.

Ja. to Candidate. Talk not to me of time or place. Now is the time and here is the place; none other will suit me. I therefore demand of you the secrets of a Master Mason.

S. D. to Ja. I cannot give them.

Ja. to Candidate. Grand Master Hiram, for the third and last time I demand of you the secrets of a Master Mason.

S. D. to Ja. Craftsman, I cannot and I will not give them.

Jubela now strikes the candidate a blow across the throat with the twenty-four inch gauge. The Senior Deacon hurries him away a short distance towards the West, where he is accosted by a brother (usually the Senior Warden) representing Jubelo, who says:

Jubelo to Candidate. Grand Master Hiram, most of the craft are waiting, and many are exceedingly anxious to receive the secrets of a Master Mason; and we can see no good reason why we are put off so long. And some of us have determined that we will wait no longer. I therefore demand of you the secrets of a Master Mason.

S. D. to Jo. Craftsman, why this violence? I cannot give them; nor can they be given except in the presence of Solomon King of Israel, Hiram King of Tyre, and myself.

Jo. to Candidate. Grand Master Hiram, your life is in danger; the avenues of the Temple are securely guarded, and escape is impossible! I therefore demand of you the secrets of a Master Mason.

S. D. to Jo. Craftsman, I cannot give them. Wait with patience for the proper time.

Jo. to Candidate. Grand Master Hiram, I again, and for the last time, demand of you the secrets of a Master Mason, or your life.

S. D. to Jo. My life you can have; my integrity, never!

Jubelo strikes a blow across the Candidate's breast with the square. He is then hustled away by the Senior Deacon in a direction towards the East, where he is accosted by a brother (generally the Master) representing Jubelum, who says:

Jubelum to Candidate. Grand Master Hiram, I have heard you caviling with Juebla and Jubelo From them you have escaped; but from me, never. My name is Jubelum. What I purpose that I perform. I hold in my hand an instrument of death: If you refuse me now, you do it at your peril! I say, give me the secrets of a Master Mason, or I will take your life.

S. D. to Jm. Craftsman, I have often refused you,

and shall always refuse when attacked in this manner. Your demands are vain!

Jm. to Candidate. Grand Master Hiram, I for the second time demand of you the secrets of a Master Mason.

S. D. to Jm. Craftsman, your demands are vain! I shall not give them. Wait until the Temple is completed, and then I will do my best to serve you.

Jm. to Candidate. Grand Master Hiram, I for the third and last time demand of you the secrets of a Master Mason.

S. D. to Jm. And I for the third time refuse you.

Jubelum, whose instrument of death is the setting maul, or something representing it, strikes the candidate with it on the forehead. At the same instant the latter is suddenly jerked backwards with sufficient force to throw him down, but is caught in falling so as to prevent any injury being done to him. The three ruffians then address one another as follows:

Jubela. What have we done?

Jubelo. We have slain our Grand Master Hiram Abiff! What shall we do with the body?

Jubelum. Let us carry it to a retired corner, and bury it in the rubbish of the Temple.

The candidate is carried to a corner of the Lodge and covered over.

Jubelum. Now let us retire until low twelve, when we will meet here again.

They all three go away to the Western side of the Lodge, and after a few moments of deathlike stillness twelve strokes are made upon a bell. They

MASTER MASON, OR THIRD DEGREE.

then return, noiselessly, to the spot where the candidate is laying.

Jubela. This is the hour—
Jubelo. This is the place—
Jubelum. And here is the body. Assist me to carry it a due West course from the Temple to the brow of a hill, where I have dug a grave six feet due East and West, and six feet perpendicular, in which we will bury it.

They take up the body (the candidate) and carry it to the West side of the Lodge, depositing it with the feet to the East between the Master's and Senior Warden's stations. The lowering of the body to the floor is done by letting it down a little at a time, so as to admit of three distinct pauses during the action.

Jubelum. I will set this sprig of acacia at the head of the grave, that the place may be known should occasion require it. And now let us make our escape, by way of Joppa, out of the country.

After a short interval of perfect silence, during which the three ruffians are supposed to have reached Joppa, the following conversation takes place between Jubelum and a sea captain:

Jubelum to Captain. Is that your ship yonder?
Capt. It is.
Jubelum. Where are you bound?
Capt. To Ethiopia.
Jubelum. When do you sail?
Capt. Immediately.
Jubelum. Do you take passengers?
Capt. I do.

MASTER MASON, OR THIRD DEGREE.

Jubelum. Will you take us?

Capt. I will, if you have King Solomon's permission to leave the country. Present your passports.

Jubelum. We will pay you your demands, but we have no passports.

Capt. Then you cannot go, for I am strictly forbidden to take any of the workmen from the Temple out of the country without King Solomon's express permisson.

Jubelum *(to his companions)*. Then let us return back to the country.

There is now another short interval of perfect quiet, followed by confused noises and talking among the craft. The Master, as King Solomon, restores silence by one rap, and says:

W. M. to S. W. Brother Grand Senior Warden, why is this confusion in the Temple, and why are the craft not at their labors?

S. W. to W. M. Our Grand Master, Hiram Abiff, is missing, most excellent King Solomon, and there are no designs upon his tressel board.

W. M. That is very singular. He has even been punctual and faithful to his trust. He must be indisposed. Order strict search to be made for him through the several apartments of the Temple.

The brethren pass indiscriminately and noisily about the Lodge, as if searching, until again brought to order and silence by one rap, given by the Senior Warden, who then reports thus:

S. W. to W. M. Your orders have been obeyed, most excellent King Solomon. The several apartments of the Temple have been strictly searched,

MASTER MASON, OR THIRD DEGREE.

but our Grand Master, Hiram Abiff, cannot be found.

W. M. to S. W. I fear, then, some accident has befallen him.

An alarm is now heard at the door, which is duly inquired into by the Junior Deacon, who reports as fololws:

J. D. to W. M. Most excellent King Solomon, twelve Fellow Crafts, clothed in white gloves and aprons, crave audience of the most excellent King Solomon.

W. M. Admit them.

The twelve Fellow Crafts approach the Master's station in the East, and one of them, acting as spokesman, reports thus:

Craftsman to W. M. Most excellent King Solomon, we twelve who appear before you are clothed in white gloves and aprons in token of our innocence. We twelve, with three others, seeing the Temple about to be completed, and being desirous of receiving the secrets of a Master Mason, whereby we could travel in foreign countries and receive wages as such, entered into the horrid conspiracy of extorting them from our Grand Master, Hiram Abiff, or taking his life. But, reflecting on the atrocity of our intentions, being struck with horror, we twelve recanted; but we fear the other three have persisted in their murderous designs. And we twelve have come before you to make this confession and implore your pardon.

W. M. to Sec. Brother Grand Secretary, call the rolls of the workmen.

The Secretary calls out a list of names taken from

the book of Nehemiah, cap. x, introducing among them the names of Jubela, Jubelo and Jubelum. As the names are called they are responded to, except the three last, by the different brethren present. As no response is made to the names of the three ruffians, the Master inquires of the craftsmen if they were the three who were associated with them in the conspiracy.

Craftsmen to W. M. They are the three, most excellent King Solomon.

W. M. It is my will and pleasure that you twelve divide yourselves into parties of three, and travel, three East, three West, three North and three South, in pursuit of the ruffians.

The twelve craftsmen depart their several ways, and there is an interval of quiet, during which the three who travel West are supposed to meet a wayfaring man, and the following conversation takes place between him and one of the three craftsmen:

Craftsman to Wayfaring Man. Have you seen any strangers pass this way recently?

Wayfarer. I saw some yesterday; three, who from their appearance were workmen from the Temple.

Craftsman. Where were they going?

Wayfarer. They were seeking a passage into Ethiopia.

Craftsman. Did they obtain one?

Wayfarer. They did not.

Craftsman. What followed?

Wayfarer. They returned back into the country.

Craftsman *(to his companions)*. Let us return and report this to King Solomon.

MASTER MASON, OR THIRD DEGREE.

After a short silence, they report to the Master as follows:

Craftsman to W. M. Tidings from the West, most excellent King Solomon.

W. M. Report them.

Craftsman. We three, who pursued a due westerly course from the Temple, went until we met with a wayfaring man, of whom we inquired if he had seen any strangers pass that way; who informed us he had, three, who from their appearance were workmen from the Temple, seeking a passage into Ethiopia, but not having obtained one, had returned back into the country. Deeming this of great importance, we have returned to bring this information to you, most excellent King Solomon.

W. M. Your intelligence proves but one thing to me, viz., that these ruffians are still in the country, and within our power. You will divide yourselves as before, and travel as before. I now give you positive injunctions to find these criminals, and as positive assurance that if you do not you yourselves will be deemed the murderers, and shall suffer for the enormous crime.

They depart westwards, and there is another short interval of silence and quiet, when the craftsman who has been acting throughout as spokesman is heard to say that he is weary and must sit down to rest and refresh himself. He sits down near the head of the candidate. He is then advised by his two companions to arise and pursue the journey; and, in rising, he grasps the sprig of acacia to assist him, which easily giving way, he calls in surprise

MASTER MASON, OR THIRD DEGREE.

the attention of his companions to the singular occurrence.

Immediately after a voice is heard in a corner of the Lodge, saying mournfully:

Jubela. Oh that my throat had been cut from ear to ear, my tongue torn out by its roots, and buried in the sands of the sea at low water mark, where the tide ebbs and flows twice in twenty-four hours, ere I had been accessory to the death of so great and good a man as our Grand Master, Hiram Abiff.

The three craftsmen whisper to each other that it is the voice of Jubela. After which Jubelo's voice is heard as follows:

Jubelo. Oh that my left breast had been torn open, my heart plucked from thence and given to the beasts of the field and the birds of the air as a prey, ere I had been accessory to the death of so great and good a man as our Grand Master, Hiram Abiff.

The three craftsmen whisper to one another that this is the voice of Jubelo. Then Jubelum's voice is heard, hoarsely exclaiming:

Jubelum. It was I that gave the fatal blow It was I that slew him Oh! that my body had been severed in twain, my bowels taken from thence and burned to ashes, and these scattered before the four winds of heaven, that no more remembrance might be had among men or Masons of so vile a wretch as I am, ere I had been accessory to the death of so great and good a man as our Grand Master, Hiram Abiff.

MASTER MASON, OR THIRD DEGREE.

The three craftsmen now consult together as follows:

1st Craftsman. What shall we do? These are the murderers of whom we are in search.

2d Craftsman. They are desperate men. It will be a serious undertaking to capture these murderers.

3d Craftsman. There are but three of them, and there are three of us. We have truth and justice on our side and our trust is in God. Let us rush in, seize, bind, and take them before King Solomon.

This being agreed upon, they do as proposed, and bring the culprits with them to the Master, where the spokesman reports as follows:

Craftsman to W. M. Tidings from the West, most excellent King Solomon.

W. M. Report them.

Craftsman. As we three, who had pursued a due westerly course from the Temple, were returning, one of us, being more weary than the rest, sat down on the brow of a hill to rest and refresh himself; and, on rising up, caught hold of a sprig of acacia, which easily giving way excited his curiosity; and, while we were meditating on this singular circumstance, we heard three frightful exclamations from the cleft of an adjacent rock. The first was the voice of Jubela, exclaiming: "Oh! that my throat had been cut from ear to ear, my tongue torn out its roots, and buried in the sands of the sea at low water mark, where the tide ebbs and flows twice in twenty-four hours, ere I had been accessory to the death of so great and good a man as our Grand Master, Hiram Abiff." The second was the voice of

MASTER MASON, OR THIRD DEGREE.

Jueblo, exclaiming: "Oh that my left breast had been torn open, my heart plucked from thence and given to the beasts of the field and the birds of the air as a prey, ere I had been accessory to the death of so great and good a man as our Grand Master, Hiram Abiff." The third was the voice of Jubelum, exclaiming more horridly than the rest: "It was I that gave the fatal blow! It was I that slew him! Oh that my body had been severed in twain, my bowels taken from thence and burned to ashes, and these scattered before the four winds of heaven, that no more remembrance might be had among men or Masons of so vile a wretch as I am, ere I had been accessory to the death of so great and good a man as our Grand Master, Hiram Abiff." Upon which we rushed in, seized, bound, and have brought them before you, most excellent King Solomon.

W. M. to Jubela. Jubela, are you guilty of this horrid deed?

Jubela. I am guilty, most excellent King Solomon.

W. M. to Jubelo. Jubelo, are you also guilty?

Jubelo. I am indeed guilty, most excellent King Solomon.

W. M. to Jubelum. Jubelum, are you likewise guilty?

Jubelum. I am most guilty, most excellent King Solomon. Yes, I am more guilty than the rest!

W. M. *(to Ruffians).* Then you shall die! Impious wretches To conspire against the life of so good and great a man as your Grand Master, Hiram Abiff. *(To the three Craftsmen.)* Take them without the gates of the city and execute them according to their several imprecations.

MASTER MASON, OR THIRD DEGREE.

The three craftsmen conduct the ruffians out of the Lodge, and a noise is made outside as if the execution was being done. After which the three craftsmen return into the Lodge, and their spokesman reports as follows:

Craftsman to W. M. Most excellent King Solomon, your orders have been obeyed. The murderers have been put to death agreeably to their several imprecations.

W. M. It is well. Go now, you twelve craftsmen, in search of the body of your Grand Master, Hiram Abiff; and, if found, observe whether the Master's Word, or a key to it, is on or about it.

The twelve now repair to the grave, make the Penal sign over it, uncover the body, and take off the jewel. They then return and report:

Craftsman to W. M. Most excellent King Solomon, your orders have been obeyed. We traveled a due westerly course from the Temple, and on the brow of the hill where our weary brother sat down to rest and refresh himself, we discovered the appearance of a newly-made grave. This we opened and discovered a body, but in so mangled a condition that it could not be raised; nor could the Master's Word or a key to it, be found on or about it. However, we found this jewel upon its breast, which we removed and have brought to you.

W. M. to S. W. Brother Grand Senior Warden, this is the jewel of the Grand Master, Hiram Abiff. No doubt can now remain as to his lamentable fate. *(To the twelve Craftsmen.)* Craftsmen, the pardon you seek for I now give you, in token of my appre-

MASTER MASON, OR THIRD DEGREE.

ciation of your endeavors to detect the murderers and to discover the body of your Grand Master, Hiram Abiff.

The twelve Craftsmen now take their seats, and the Master continues as follows:

W. M. to S. W. Brother Grand Senior Warden, you will form the craft in grand procession, to go with me to endeavor to raise the body of the Grand Master, Hiram Abiff. And as the Master's Word is now lost, it is my will and pleasure that the first sign given at the grave, and the first word spoken after the body shall be raised, shall be adopted for the regulation of all Master Masons' Lodges until future ages shall find out the right.

S. W. to Lodge. Craftsmen, form yourselves in grand procession to go with the most excellent King Solomon to endeavor to raise the body of the Grand Master, Hiram Abiff.

They are formed, two by two, in procession; and, singing the funeral dirge, they march around the body, leaving it on their right. The Senior Warden marches behind them, and the Master closes the procession last of all. Meanwhile the Senior Deacon removes the hoodwink from the candidate. The procession passes three times around the body, and halts with the Master standing at the head of the body and the Senior Warden on the right. The Master and the craft all give the Penal sign, and the Master makes the following address:

W. M. Here, then, lie the remains of your Grand Master, Hiram Abiff. Stricken down in the performance of duty; a martyr to his fidelity, he was

MASTER MASON, OR THIRD DEGREE.

borne to this lonely spot by unhallowed hands at a midnight hour, under the hope that the eye of man would never more find him, nor the hand of justice be laid upon his guilty murderers. Vain hope. Here lie the remains of your Grand Master, Hiram Abiff His work was not done, yet his column is broken! The honors so justly his due have not been paid him. His death was untimely and his brethren mourn! His body shall be raised; shall be honored; shall be borne to the Temple for more decent interment; and a monument shall be erected to commemorate his labors, his fidelity and his untimely death. Brother Grand Senior Warden, apply to the body the grip of the Eternal Apprentice, and endeavor to raise it.

The Senior Warden obeys, and reports:

S. W. Most excellent King Solomon, your order has been obeyed, but the body is putrid, it having been dead fifteen days; the skin slips from the flesh, and it cannot be so raised.

The Master then makes the grand hailing sign of distress once, with the appropriate words, which is imitated by the craft.

W. M. to S. W. Brother Grand Senior Warden, you have a stronger grip, the grip of the Fellow Craft. Apply to the body that grip and endeavor to raise it.

The Senior Warden again obeys, and reports:

S. W. to W. M. Most excellent King Solomon, your order has been obeyed, but the flesh cleaves from the bone, and it cannot be so raised.

The grand hailing sign of distress is repeated as before, and the Master continues:

MASTER MASON, OR THIRD DEGREE.

W. M. to S. W. Brother Grand Senior Warden, our attempts are vain! What shall we do?

S. W. Pray.

The brethren all stand with folded arms, while the Master offers the following prayer:

Thou, O God! knowest our downsitting and our uprising, and understandest our thought afar off. Shield and defend us from the evil intentions of our enemies, and support us under the trials and afflictions we are destined to endure while traveling through this vale of tears. Man that is born of woman is of few days and full of trouble. He cometh forth as a flower, and is cut down; he fleeth also as a shadow, and continueth not. Seeing his days are deterinmed, the number of his months are with thee, thou has appointed his bounds that he cannot pass; turn from him that he may rest, till he shall accomplish his day. For there is hope of a tree, if it be cut down, that it will sprout again, and that the tender branch thereof will not cease. But man dieth and wasteth away; yea, man giveth up the ghost, and where is he? As the water fail from the sea, and the flood decayeth and drieth up, so man lieth down, and riseth not up till the heavens shall be no more. Yet, O Lord! have compassion on the children of thy creation, administer them comfort in time of trouble, and save them with an everlasting salvation. *Amen. So mote it be.*

After a short pause at the conclusion of the prayer, the Master says:

W. M. to S. W. Brother Grand Senior Warden, your counsel was timely and good. Masons should

MASTER MASON, OR THIRD DEGREE.

ever remember that when the strength and wisdom of man fails, there is an inexhaustible supply above, yielded to us through the power of prayer. My mind is now clear, and the body shall be raised. *(To the Craft.)* Craftsmen, you have labored upon the Temple more than seven years, honestly toiling, encouraged and buoyed up by the promise that when the Temple was completed those of you who were faithful should receive the secrets of a Master Mason. The Master's Word is lost in the death of your Grand Master, Hiram Abiff. But I will substitute a word, which shall be adopted for the regulation of all Master Masons' Lodges until future ages shall find out the right. And the first word I uttter when the body is raised from a dead level to a living perpendicular shall be such substituted word. Yea, my brethren, I have a word; and though the skin may slip from the flesh, and the flesh cleave from the bone, there is strength in the Lion of the Tribe of Judah ,and he shall prevail.

The Master now changes his position to the feet of the candidate; he places his right foot firmly against them, and taking the candidate by the strong grip of a Master Mason, or Lion's Paw, he raises him up, aided by the Senior Warden and Senior Deacon. He then, on the five points of fellowship, whispers the Grand Masonic Word in the candidate's ear, and requires him to return it in the same manner. The Master next explains to him the strong grip of a Master Mason, which he follows with the explanation of the five points of fellowship, as follows:

W. M. The five points of fellowship are foot to

MASTER MASON, OR THIRD DEGREE.

foot, knee to knee, breast to breast, hand to back, and cheek to cheek or mouth to ear. Foot to foot, that we will never hesitate to go on foot, and out of our way, to aid and succor a needy brother; knee to knee, that we will ever remember a brother's welfare in all our applications to Deity; breast to breast, that we will ever keep in our breasts a brother's secret, when communicated as such, murder and treason excepted; hand to back, that we will ever be ready to stretch forth our hand to aid and support a fallen brother; cheek to cheek or mouth to ear, that we will ever whisper good counsel in the ear of a brother, and in the most tender manner remind him of his faults, and endeavor to aid his reformation, and will give him due and timely notice, that he may ward off all approaching danger.

The Master next explains to the candidate the grand hailing sign of distress, and then resumes his station in the East, the candidate being conducted to a position at the right hand of the Master, who proceeds to deliver the following charge:

W. M. to Candidate: Brother, your zeal for the institution of Masonry, the progress you have made in the mystery, and your conformity to our regulations, have pointed you out as a proper object of our favor and esteem.

You are now bound by duty, honor and gratitude to be faithful to your trust; to support the dignity of your character on every occasion; and to enforce, by precept and example, obedience to the tenets of the Order.

In the character of a Master Mason, you are au-

MASTER MASON, OR THIRD DEGREE.

thorized to correct the errors and irregularities of your uninformed brethren, and to guard them against a breach of fidelity. To preserve the reputation of the Fraternity unsullied must be your constant care; and for this purpose it is your province to recommend to your inferiors obedience and submission; to your equals, courtesy and affability; to your superiors, kindness and condescension. Universal benevolence you are always to inculcate; and, by the regularity of your own behavior, afford the best example for the conduct of others less informed. The ancient landmarks of the Order, intrusted to your care, you are carefully to preserve, and never suffer them to be infringed, or countenance a deviation from the established usages and customs of the Fraternity.

Your virtue, honor and reputation are concerned in supporting with dignity the character you now bear. Let no motive, therefore, make you swerve from your duty, violate your vows, or betray your trust; but be true and faithful, and imitate the example of that celebrated artist whom you this evening represent. Thus you will render yourself deserving of the honor which we have conferred upon, and merit the confidence that we have reposed in, you.

At the conclusion of the charge the Master takes his seat, and then seats the Lodge by one rap; and the newly-made Master Mason is seated in front of the Master during the rehearsal of the entire lecture of the third degree by the Master, assisted by the Senior Warden.

MASTER MASON, OR THIRD DEGREE.

LECTURE OF THE THIRD DEGREE.

SECTION I.

W. M. Are you a Master Mason?

S. W. I am.

W. M. What induced you to become a Master Mason?

S. W. In order that I might receive Masters' wages, and better to be enabled to support myself and family, and contribute to the relief of poor, distressed Master Masons, their widows and orphans.

W. M. Where were you made a Master Mason?

S. W. In a just and lawfully constituted Lodge of Master Masons.

W. M. How were you prepared?

S. W. By being divested of all metals, neither naked nor clothed, barefoot nor shod, hoodwinked, and a cable-tow three times about my naked body, in which situation I was conducted to the door of the Lodge by a brother.

W. M. Why had you a cable-tow three times about your naked body

S. W. It was to signify that my duties and obligations became more and more extensive as I advanced in Masonry.

W. M. How gained you admission?

S. W. By three distinct knocks.

W. M. What was said to you from within?

S. W. Who comes here?

W. M. Your answer?

S. W. A brother who has been regularly initiated as an Entered Apprentice, passed to the degree of a

MASTER MASON, OR THIRD DEGREE.

Fellow Craft, and now wishes to receive further light in Masonry by being raised to the sublime degree of a Master Mason.

W. M. What were you then asked?

S. W. If it was of my own free will and accord; if I was duly and truly prepared; worthy and well qualified; if I had made suitable proficiency in the preceding degrees; all of which being answered in the affirmative, I was asked by what further right or benefit I expected to gain admission.

W. M. Your answer?

S. W. By the benefit of the pass.

W. M. Did you give the pass?

S. W. I gave it not; my guide gave it for me.

W. M. What followed?

S. W. I was directed to wait with patience until the Worshipful Master was informed of my request and his answer returned.

W. M. What answer did he return?

S. W. Let him enter and be received in due form.

W. M. How were you received?

S. W. On both points of the compasses, extending from my naked right to left breasts, which was to signify that as the vital parts of man are contained within the breasts, so the most useful tenets of our institution are contained withn the two points of the compasses, which are friendship, morality and brotherly love.

W. M. How were you then disposed of?

S. W. I was conducted three times about the altar to the Junior Warden in the South, where the same

MASTER MASON, OR THIRD DEGREE.

questions were asked and like answers returned as at the door.

W. M. How did the Junior Warden dispose of you?

S. W. He directed me to the Senior Warden in the West, where the same questions were asked and like answers returned as before.

W. M. How did the Senior Warden dispose of you?

S. W. He directed me to the Worshipful Master in the East, where the same questions were asked and like answers returned as before.

W. M. What did the Worshipful Master demand of you?

S. W. From whence I came and whither I was traveling?

W. M. Your answer?

S. W. From the West and traveling to the East.

W. M. What did he further demand of you?

S. W. What I was in pursuit of.

W. M. Your answer?

S. W. That which was lost; which, by my endeavors and his assistance, I was in hopes to find.

W. M. What did he further demand of you?

S. W. To what I referred.

W. M. Your answer?

S. W. To the secrets of a Master Mason; after which he observed that my pursuit was truly laudable, and ordered me to be reconducted to the Senior Warden in the West, who taught me to approach to the East, advancing by three upright, regular steps, my feet forming the right angle of a perfect square,

MASTER MASON, OR THIRD DEGREE.

my body erect to the Worshipful Master in the East.

W. M. What did the Worshipful Master then do with you?

S. W. He made me a Master Mason.

W. M. How?

S. W. In due form.

W. M. What is the due form?

S. W. Kneeling on my naked knees; my body erect; my naked hands resting on the Holy Bible, square and compasses; in which due form I took the obligation of a Master Mason.

W. M. Repeat it.

S. W. I, A. B., of my own free will ,etc. *(See page 152.)*

W. M. After taking the obligation, what were you then asked?

S. W. What I most desired.

W. M. Your answer

S. W. Further light in Masonry.

W. M. Did you receive it?

S. W. I did.

W. M. How?

S. W. By order of the Worshipful Master and assistance of the brethren.

W. M. On being brought to light, what did you first dscover more than you had heretofore discovered?

S. W. Both points of the compasses bare, which was to teach me never to lose sight of the Masonic application of this useful and valuable instrument, which teaches friendship, morality and brotherly love

MASTER MASON, OR THIRD DEGREE.

W. M. What did you then discover?

S. W. The Worshipful Master approaching me from the East, under the due guard and sign of a Master Mason, who, in token of the further continuance of his brotherly love and favor, presented me with his right hand, and with it the pass and token of the pass of a Master Mason, and bid me arise and salute the Wardens as such.

W. M. After saluting the Wardens, what did you then discover?

S. W. The Worshipful Master, who ordered me to the Senior Warden, who taught me how to wear my apron as a Master Mason.

W. M. After being taught to wear your apron as a Master Mason, how were you then disposed of?

S. W. I was conducted to the right hand of the Worshipful Master in the East, who presented me with the working tools of a Master Mason, and taught me their uses.

W. M. What are the working tools of a Master Mason?

S. W. All the implements of Masonry indiscriminately, but more especially the trowel.

W. M. What is the use of the towel?

S. W. The trowel is an instrument made use of by operative masons to spread the cement which unites a building into one common mass; but we, as Free and Accepted Masons, are taught to make use of it for the more noble and glorious purpose of spreading the cement of brotherly love and affection; that cement which unites us into one sacred band, or society of friends and brothers, among whom no con-

MASTER MASON, OR THIRD DEGREE.

tention should ever exist but that noble contention, or rather emulation, of who best can work or best agree.

W. M. How were you then disposed of?

S. W. I was ordered to be reconducted to the place from whence I came, there be reinvested of what I had been divested, and await the Worshipful Master's will and pleasure.

SECTION II.

W. M. What does a Master Masons' Lodge represent?

S. W. The Sanctum Sanctorum, or Holy of Holies, of King Solomon's Temple.

W. M. Did you ever return to the Lodge?

S. W. I did.

W. M. On your return, where were you placed?

S. W. In the centre; there caused to kneel, and implore the blessing of Deity.

W. M. What followed?

S. W. I arose; and on my passage about the altar was accosted by three Fellow Crafts, who thrice demanded of me the secrets of a Master Mason, and on being thrice refused, the first gave me a blow with the twenty-four inch gauge across my throat, the second with the square across my breast, the third with the setting maul on my forehead, which felled me on the spot.

W. M. Who did you then represent?

S. W. Our Grand Master, Hiram Abiff, who was slain just before the completion of the Temple.

W. M. Was his death premeditated?

MASTER MASON, OR THIRD DEGREE.

S. W. It was, by fifteen Fellow Crafts, who, seeing the Temple about to be completed, and being desirous of receiving the secrets of a Master Mason, whereby they could travel in foreign countries and receive wages as such, entered into the horrid conspiracy of extorting them from our Grand Master, Hiram Abiff, or taking his life; but, reflecting on the atrocity of their intentions, being struck with horror, twelve of them recanted; the other three persisted in their murderous designs.

W. M. At what time was our Grand Master, Hiram Abiff, slain?

S. W. At high twelve.

W. M. How came he to be assassinated at that hour?

S. W. It was his usual custom at high twelve, when the craft were called from labor to refreshment, to enter into the Sanctum Sanctorum, or Holy of Holies, there offer up his adorations to Deity, and draw his designs on his tressel board.

W. M. What was the manner of his death?

S. W. The three Fellow Crafts who persisted in their murderous design, knowing this to be his usual custom, placed themselves at the South, West and East gates of the Temple, and there awaited his return.

W. M. What followed?

S. W. Our Grand Master, Hiram Abiff, having fulfilled his usual custom, attempted to return by the South gate, where he was accosted by Jubela, who demanded of him the secrets of a Master Mason; and, on being refused, gave him a blow

MASTER MASON, OR THIRD DEGREE.

with the twenty-four inch gauge across his throat; upon which he fled, and attempted to pass out at the West gate, where he was accosted by Jubelo, who in like manner thrice demanded of him the secrets of a Master Mason; and, on his thrice refusing; gave him a blow with the square across his breast; upon which he fled, and attempted to make his escape at the East gate, when he was accosted by Jubelum, who in like manner thrice demanded of him the secrets of a Master Mason; and, on his thrice refusing, gave him a violent blow with the setting maul on his forehead, which felled him dead on the spot.

W. M. What did they do with the body?

S. W. Buried it in the rubbish of the Temple until low twelve, or twelve at night, when they met by agreement, and carried it a due West course from the Temple to the brow of a hill, where they buried it in a grave dug six feet due East and West and six feet perpendicular, at the head of which they set a sprig of acacia, that the place might be known should occasion ever require it, and made their escape.

W. M. At what time was our Grand Master, Hiram Abiff, first missed?

S. W. On the day following.

W. H. How was his absence discovered?

S. W. By there being no designs upon his tressel board.

W. M. What followed?

S. W. King Solomon, being informed of this, supposed him to be indisposed, ordered strict search

MASTER MASON, OR THIRD DEGREE.

to be made for him through the several apartments of the Temple. Search was accordingly made, but he could not be found.

W. M. What followed?

S. W. King Solomon then feared some accident had befallen him, and ordered the rolls of the workmen to be called; and on roll call there were found three Fellow Crafts' missing.

W. M. What followed

S. W. The twelve Fellow Crafts who had recanted from their murderous designs presented themselves before King Solomon, clothed in white gloves and aprons, in token of their innocence, confessed their premeditated guilt and implored his pardon.

W. M. What followed?

S. W. King Solomon ordered them to divide themselves into parties of three, and travel, three East, three West, three North and three South, in pursuit of the ruffians.

W. M. What followed?

S. W. The twelve divided; and those who pursued a due westerly course from the Temple went until they met with a wayfaring man, of whom they inquired if he had seen any strangers pass that way; who informed them that he had, three, who from their appearance were workmen from the Temple, seeking a passage into Ethiopia, but not having obtained one, had returned back into the country.

W. M. What followed?

S. W. They returned, and brought the intelligence to King Solomon, who ordered them to divide themselves as before and travel as before, with positive injunctions to find the criminals, and with as positive assurance that if they did not them themselves would be deemed the murderers and severally suffer for their enormous crime.

W. M. What followed?

S. W. They traveled as before; and those who had pursued a due westerly course from the Temple were returning; one of them, being more weary than the rest, sat down on the brow of a hill to rest and refresh himself, and on rising up caught hold of a sprig of acacia, which easily giving way excited his curiosity; and while they were meditating on this singular circumstance, they heard three frightful exclamations from the cleft of an adjacent rock. The first was the voice of Jubela, exclaiming: Oh! that my throat had been cut from ear to ear, my tongue, etc. *(See page 169.)* The second was the voice of Jubelo, examining: Oh! that my left breast had been torn open, my heart, etc. *(See page 169.)* The third was the voice of Jubelum, exclaiming more hoarsely than the rest: It was I that gave the fatal blow! It was I that slew him! Oh! that my body had been severed in twain, my bowels, etc. *(See page 169.)* Upon which they rushed in, seized, bound and brought them before King Solomon, who ordered them to be taken without the gates of the city and executed according to their imprecations. They were accordingly put to death.

W. M What followed?

S. W. King Solomon ordered the twelve Fellow Crafts to go in search of the body, and, if found, to observe whether the Master's Word, or a key to it, was on or about it.

MASTER MASON, OR THIRD DEGREE.

W. M. Where was the body of our Grand Master, Hiram Abiff, found?

S. W. A due westerly course from the Temple, on the brow of the hill where our weary brother sat down to rest and refresh himself.

W. M. Was the Master's Word, or a key to it, on or about it

S. W. It was not.

W. M. What followed?

S. W. King Solomon then ordered them to go with him to raise the body; and ordered that, as the Master's Word was then lost, the first sign given at the grave, and the first word spoken after the body should be raised, should be adopted for the regulation of all Master Mason's Lodges until future ages should find out the right.

W. M. What followed?

S. W. They returned to the grave, where King Solomon ordered them to take the body by the Entered Apprentice grip, and see if it could be raised; but on taking the body it was so putrid, it having been dead fifteen days, the skin slipped from the flesh, and it could not be so raised.

W. M. What followed?

S. W. King Solomon then ordered them to take it by the Fellow Crafts grip, and see if it could be so raised; but on taking the body by this grip, the flesh cleft from the bone, and it could not be so raised.

W. M. What followed?

S. W. King Solomon then took it by the strong grip of a Master Mason or Lion's Paw, and raised it

MASTER MASON, OR THIRD DEGREE.

on the five points of fellowship, which are foot to foot, knee to knee, breast to breast, hand to back, cheek to cheek or mouth to ear. Foot to foot, that we will never hesitate to go, etc. *(See page 177)*.... that he may ward off all approaching danger.

W. M. What did they then do with the body?

S. W. They carried it to the Temple, and buried it in due form. And Masonic tradition informs us that there was a marble column erected to his memory, upon which was delineated a beautiful virgin weeping; before her lay a book open, in her right hand a sprig of acacia, in her left an urn, and behind her stood Time, with his fingers unfolding the ringlets of her hair.

W. M. What do these hieroglyphic figures denote?

S. W. The broken column denotes the untimely death of our Grand Master, Hiram Abiff; the beautiful virgin weeping the Temple unfinished; the book open before her, that his virtues lie there on perpetual record; the sprig of acacia in her right hand, the timely discovery of his body; the urn in her left, that his ashes were there safely deposited to perpetuate the remembrance of so distinguished a character; Time unfolding the ringlets of her hair, that time, patience and perseverance accomplish all things.

W. M. Have you any signs belonging to this degree

S. W. I have several.

W. M. Give me a sign.

The Senior Warden makes the Penal sign.

MASTER MASON. OR THIRD DEGREE.

W. M. What is that called?
S. W. The due guard of a Master Mason.
W. M. Has that an allusion?
S. W. It has, to the penalty of my obligation; and when our ancient brethren returned to the grave of our Grand Master, Hiram Abiff, they found their hands placed in this position, to guard their nostrils from the disagreeable effluvium that arose there from the grave.
W. M. Give me a token.
The Senior Warden gives it.
W. M. What is that called?
S. W. The pass-grip from a Fellow Craft to a Master Mason.
W. M. What is its name.
The Senior Warden gives the name.
W. M. Who was......?
S. W. The first known artificer or cunning worker in metals.
W. M. Pass that.
The Senior Warden giveh the strong grip.
W. M. What is that?
S. W. The strong grip of a Master Mason or Lion's Paw.
W. M. Has this a name?
S. W. It has.
W. M. Will you give it to me?
S. W. I will if you place yourself in a proper position.
W. M. What is that proper position?
S. W. The five points of fellowship.
W. M. Advance and give it. *(The Senior Warden obeys.)* The word is right.

MASTER MASON, OR THIRD DEGREE.

W. M. How many Grand Masonic Pillars are there?

S. W. Three.

W. M. What are they called?

S. W. Wisdom, Strength and Beauty.

W. M. Why are they so called?

S. W. Because it is necessary there should be wisdom to contrive, strength to support, and beauty to adorn all great and important undertakings.

W. M. By whom are they represented?

S. W. By Solomon King of Israel, Hiram King of Tyre, and Hiram Abiff, who were our first three most excellent Grand Masters.

W. M. Why are they said to represent them?

S. W. Solomon King of Israel represents the Pillar of Wisdom, because by his wisdom he contrived the superb model of excellence that immortalized his name; Hiram King of Tyre represents the Pillar of Strength, because he supported King Solomon in that great and important undertaking; Hiram Abiff represents the Pillar of Beauty, because of his cunning workmanship the Temple was beautified and adorned.

W. M. What supported the Temple?

S. W. It was supported by one thousand four hundred and fifty-three columns, and two thousand nine hundred and six pilasters, all hewn from the finest Parian marble.

W. M. How many were employed in building the Temple

S. W. Three Grand Masters, three thousand three hundred Masters, or overseers of the work, eighty

MASTER MASON, OR THIRD DEGREE.

thousand Fellow Crafts in the mountains and in the quarries, and seventy thousand Entered Apprentices, or bearers of burthens. All these were classed and arranged in such a manner by the wisdom of King Solomon, that neither envy, discord nor confusion were suffered to interrupt that universal peace and tranquility which pervaded the world at this important period.

W. M. What is meant by the three steps usually delineated on the Master's carpet?

S. W. They are emblematical of the three principal stages of human life, viz., youth, manhood and age. In youth, as Entered Apprentices, we ought industriously to occupy our minds in the attainment of useful knowledge; in manhood, as Fellow Crafts, we should apply our knowledge to the discharge of our respective duties to God, our neighbors and ourselves; that so in age, as Master Masons, we may enjoy the happy reflections consequent on a well-spent life, and die in the hope of a glorious immortality.

W. M. How many classes of Master's emblems are there?

S. W. Nine. The Pot of Incence is an emblem of a pure heart, which is always an acceptable sacrifice to the Deity; and, as this glows with fervent heat, so should our hearts continually glow with gratitude to the great and beneficent Author of our existence, for the manifold blessings and comforts we enjoy.

The Bee-hive is an emblem of industry, and recommends the practice of that virtue to all created beings, from the highest seraph in heaven

MASTER MASON, OR THIRD DEGREE.

to the lowest reptile of the dust. It teaches us that as we came into the world rational and intelligent beings, so we should ever be industrious ones; never sitting down contented while our fellow-creatures around us are in want, when it is in our power to relieve them without inconvenience to ourselves.

When we take a survey of nature, we view man, in his infancy, more helpless and indigent than the brutal creation; he lies languishing for days, months and years, totally incapable of providing sustenance for himself, of guarding against the attack of the wild beasts of the field, or shelting hmself from the inclemencies of the weather.

It might have pleased the great Creator of heaven and earth to have made man independent of all other beings; but, as dependence is one of the strongest bonds of society, mankind were made dependent on each other for protection and security, as they thereby enjoy better opportunities of fulfilling the duties of reciprocal love and friendship. Thus was man formed for social and active life, the noblest part of the work of God; and he that will so demean himself as not to be endeavoring to add to the common stock of knowledge and understanding, may be deemed a drone in the hive of nature, a useless member of society, and unworthy of our protection as Masons.

The Book of Constitutions, guarded by the Tyler's sword, reminds us that we should be ever watchful and guarded in our thoughts, words and actions, particularly when before the enemies of Masonry; ever bearing in remembrance those truly Masonic virtues, silence and circumspection.

MASTER MASON, OR THIRD DEGREE.

The Sword, pointing to a naked heart, demonstrates that justice will sooner or later overtake us; and although our thoughts, words and actions may be hidden from the eyes of man, yet that All-seeing Eye, whom the sun, moon and stars obey, and under whose watchful care even comets perform their stupendous revolutions, pervades the inmost recesses of the human heart, and will reward us according to our merits.

The Anchor and Ark are emblems of a well-grounded hope and a well-spent life. They are emblematical of that divine ark which safely wafts us over this tempestuous sea of troubles, and that anchor which shall safely moor us in a peaceful harbor, where the wicked cease from troubling and the weary shall find rest.

The Forty-seventh Problem of Euclid—this was an invention of our ancient friend and brother, the great Pythagoras, who, in his travels through Asia, Africa and Europe, was initiated into several orders of priesthood, and raised to the sublime degree of a Master Mason. This wise philosopher enriched his mind abundantly in a general knowledge of things, and more especially in Geometry, or Masonry: on this subject he drew out many problems and theorems; and among the most distinguished he erected this, which, in the joy of his heart, he called Eureka, in the Grecian language signifying, I have found it; and upon the discovery of which he is said to have sacrificed a hecatomb.

It teaches Masons to be general lovers of the arts and science.

MASTER MASON, OR THIRD DEGREE.

The Hour-glass is an emblem of human life. Behold! how swiftly the sands run, and how rapidly our lives are drawing to a close. We cannot without astonishment behold the little particles which are contained in this machine, how they pass away almost imperceptibly, and yet, to our surpise, in the short space of an hour they are all exhausted. Thus wastes man! To-day, he puts forth the tender leaves of hope: to-morrow, blossoms, and bears his blushing honors thick upon him; the next day comes a frost, which nips the shoot, and when he thinks his greatness is still aspiring, he falls, like autumn leaves, to enrich our mother earth.

The Scythe is an emblem of time, which cuts the brittle thread of life, and launches us into eternity. Behold! what havoc the scythe of time makes among the human race; if, by chance, we should escape the numerous evils incident to childhood and youth, and with health and vigor arrive to the years of manhood, yet, withal, we must soon be cut down by the all-devouring scythe of time, and be gathered into the land where our fathers have gone before us.

(In many instances the entire explantory matter contained in the above answer is omitted, the reply to the foregoing question being simply "Nine.")

W. M. What is the ninth?

S. W. The setting maul, spade, coffin and sprig of acacia. The setting maul is that by which our Grand Master, Hiram Abiff, was slain; the spade was that which dug his grave; the coffin was that which received his remans; and the sprig of acacia was that which bloomed at the head of his grave.

MASTER MASON, OR THIRD DEGREE.

These are all striking emblems of mortality, and afford serious reflections to a thinking mind; but they would be still more gloomy were it not for the sprig of acacia that bloomed at the head of the grave, which serves to remind us of that imperishable part of man which survives the grave, and bears the nearest affinity to the supreme intelligence which pervades all nature, and which can never, never, never die. Then, finally, my brethren, let us imitate our Grand Master, Hiram Abiff, in his virtuous conduct, his unfeigned piety to God, and his inflexible fidelity to his trust; that, like him, we may welcome the grim tyrant, Death, and receive him as a kind messenger sent by our Supreme Grand Master to translate us from this imperfect to that all-perfect, glorious and celestial Lodge above, where the Supreme Architect of the Universe presides.

After the lecture the new brother takes his seat among the other brethren.

CLOSING A LODGE OF MASTER MASONS.

W. M. to S. W. Brothern Senior Warden, have you anything in the West to come before this Lodge of Master Masons?

S. W. Nothing in the West, Worshipful Master.

W. M. to J. W. Anything in the South, brother Junior Warden?

J. W. Nothing in the South, Worshipful Master.

W. M. to Sec. Brother Secretary, have you anything on your table?

Sec. Nothing, Worshipful Master.

MASTER MASON, OR THIRD DEGREE.

W. M. to J. D. Brother Junior Deacon, what is the last great care of Masons when in Lodge assembled

J. D. To see that the Lodge is duly tyled, Worshipful Master.

W. M. Perform that duty, and inform the Tyler that I am about to close this Lodge of Master Masons.

The Junior Deacon opens the door and communicates the Master's order, and reports:

J. D. to W. M. The Lodge is duly tyled, Worshipful Master.

W. M. How are we tyled, brother Junior Deacon?

J. D. By a brother Master Mason without the door, armed with the proper instrument of his office.

W. M. What are his duties there?

J. D. To keep off all cowans and eavesdroppers, and to see that none pass or repass but such as are duly qualified and have permission from the Worshipful Master.

The Worshipful Master now seats the Deacons by one rap.

W. M. to S. W. Are you a Master Mason?

S. W. I am.

W. M. What induced you to become a Master Mason?

S. W. In order that I might receive Masters' wages, and better to be enabled to support myself and family, and contribute to the relief of poor, distressed Master Masons, their widows and orphans.

W. M. Where were you made a Master Mason?

S. W. In a just and lawfully constituted Lodge of Master Masons.

MASTER MASON, OR THIRD DEGREE.

W. M. How many anciently composed a Lodge of Master Masons?

S. W. Three of more.

W. M. When composed of only three, who were they?

S. W. The Worshipful Master, Senior Warden and Junior Warden.

W. M. What is the Junior Warden's station in the Lodge?

S. W. In the South.

W. M. to J. W. Why are you in the South, brother Junior Warden? What are your duties there?

J. W. to W. M. As the Sun in the South at its meridian height is the glory and beauty of the day, so stands the Junior Warden in the South, the better to observe the time; to call the craft from labor to refreshment; to superintend them during the hours thereof, and see that they do not convert the purposes of refreshment into intemperance and excess; to call them on again in due season, that the Worshipful Master may have pleasure and the craft profit thereby.

W. M. to J. W. What is the Senior Warden's station in the Lodge?

J. W. In the West.

W. M. to S. W. Why are you in the West, brother Senior Warden? What are your duties there?

S. W. to W. M. As the Sun is in the West at the close of the day, so is the Senior Warden in the West to assist the Worshipful Master in opening and closing his Lodge; to pay the craft their wages, if any be due, and see that none go away dissatis-

MASTER MASON, OR THIRD DEGREE.

fled, harmony being the strength and support of all societies, more especially of our.

W. M. to S. W. What is the Worshipful Master's station in the Lodge?

S. W. to W. M. In the East.

W. M. to S. W. Why is he in the East, brother Senior Warden? What are his duties there?

S. W. to W. M. As the Sun rises in the East to open and govern the day, so rises the Worshipful Master in the East to open and govern his Lodge, to set the craft to work, and give them good and wholesome instruction for their labors.

The Master calls up the Lodge by three raps.

W. M. to S. W. Brother Senior Warden, it is my will and pleasure that ———— Lodge number ———— be now closed. Communicate this order to the Junior Warden in the South, and he to the craft for their government.

S. W. to J. W. Brother Junior Warden, it is the will and pleasure of the Worshipful Master in the East that ———— Lodge number ———— be now closed; communicate this order to the craft for their government.

J. W. to Lodge. Brethren, it is the will and pleasure of the Worshipful Master in the East, communicated to me by the Senior Warden in the West, that ———— Lodge number ———— be now closed; take notice and govern yourselves accordingly.—Look to the East!

The signs are now given, the raps passed about the stations three times, and the usual prayer is offered. When this is done, the Master asks the following questions:

MASTER MASON, OR THIRD DEGREE.

W. M. to S. W. Brother Senior Warden, how do Masons meet?

S. W. Upon the level, Worshipful Master.

W. M. Brother Junior Warden, how do Masons act?

J. W. Upon the plumb, Worship Master.

W. M. to Lodge. And they part upon the square. So may we meet, act and part. May the blessings of heaven rest upon us and all regular Masons! May brotherly love prevail, and every moral and social virtue cement us! In the name of God and the Holy Saints John I declare this Lodge closed in form. Brother Junior Deacon, inform the Tyler.

The Master gives three raps and the craft are dismissed. The Junior Deacon gives three raps at the door, which are answered by the Tyler, and as soon as the Master's orders are communicated to him, the door is thrown upon for the brethren to depart.

Meanwhile the Senior Deacon closes the Great Lights, and places them on the Secretary's table, who secures them in the proper place. The Lesser Lights are removed, and the Wardens reverse their columns, down in the West, erect in the South.

THE LODGE.

A LODGE is understood to be the room or place in which a regularly constituted body of Freemasons assembles for work and the transaction of business connected with the Institution. The term is also used to designate the collection of Masons thus assembled, just as we use the word "church" to signify the building in which a congregation of worshippers meet, as well as the congregation itself.

A Lodge is defined to be an assembly of Masons, *just, perfect,* and *regular,* who together meet to expatiate on the beauties and mysteries of the Order, and to add new material to the sacred work. It is *just,* because it contains the volume of the Sacred Law unfolded, together with the square and compasses; *perfect,* having the required number of members present to transact business in a regular and constitutional manner, and *regular,* from its warrant of constitution, which implies that it meets and works under the sanction of the legal Masonic authority of the jurisdiction in which the Lodge is held, subject to its by-laws and the general regulations. It is either particular or general, and will be best understood by attending it.—*Charges of* 1722.

FORMATION OF LODGES.

No Lodge is recognized at the present day unless it has emanated from a Grand Lodge, and works in obedience to the regulations of its parent. Whatever may be the status of a Mason irregularly made, no countenance is given to an irregular (clandestine) Lodge.

Lodges, according to the American system, are recognized of two kinds, distinct in their character, and working under distinct and separate authority: the first, *Under Dispensation* from the Grand Master; the second, *Under Warrant* (charter) from the Grand Lodge. Their powers and authority will be separately considered.

LODGE UNDER DISPENSATION.

In the formation of a new Lodge, which is technically termed a *Lodge under Dispensation*, a petition signed by not less than seven Master Masons in good standing is presented to the Grand Master, or other officer having authority to grant dispensations. There must be good reason for the organization of the Lodge at that time and place. The place of meeting must be designated, and the names of the first three officers stated. The petition must be recommended by the nearest chartered Lodge (in some States all the Lodges whose territory would be reduced), which must certify that the officers proposed are qualified to confer the degrees and give the lectures, etc.

POWERS OF A LODGE UNDER DISPENSATION.

The powers of a Lodge under dispensation are such as may be prescribed by the local regulations in force in the jurisdiction where it is located. The petitioners for the new Lodge must give notice to the old Lodge that they have signed such petition, and pay all dues to that time; but (in the most of States) they are not required to dimit from the Lodge until the charter is granted. This, however, like other rules, is subject to local regulations. Usually a Lodge U. D. has the same authority as a warranted Lodge except holding elections and installing officers.

CHARTERED LODGES.

The powers, duties and privileges of a subordinate Lodge are such as are defined by its charter, by the constitutions and general regulations of the Grand Lodge, and the ancient landmarks. They are divided into—

I. EXECUTIVE.—In the direction and performance of its work under the control of its Master, and in all other matters in sustaining the Master, who has the primary executive power of the Lodge.

II. LEGISLATIVE.—Embracing all matters relating to its internal concerns not in derogation of the ancient landmarks, the constitutions and general regulations of the Grand Lodge, or of its own particular by-laws; and

III. JUDICIAL.—Embracing the exercise of discipline and settlement of controversies between and over all its members (except the Master), and over all Masons and non-affiliated brethren within its jurisdiction, subject to an appeal to the Grand Lodge.

The powers of a chartered Lodge are divided into INHERENT and CORPORATE.

A Lodge by virtue of its inherent rights, as defined by ancient landmarks, established usages of Masonry, and when recognized by a Grand Lodge, has the power: 1. To retain its charter until lawfully surrendered, suspended, or revoked; 2. To fix its time and place (if not outside of the place named in the charter) of meetings; 3. To meet and do all the work of craft Masonry; 4. To elect and initiate members, and reject any application for membership; 5. To elect and install its officers; 6. To make laws requiring its members to contribute to its funds; 7. To instruct its representatives, for their government, at all communications of the Grand Lodge; 8. To place on trial, for cause, its own members, sojourners, and unaffiliated Masons living within its jurisdiction; 9. To appeal to the Grand Master or Grand Lodge from the decision of the Master; 10. To make by-laws for its local government.

The corporate rights of a Lodge are conferred by its charter, and by the powers thereof they are entitled: 1. To representation in all communications of the Grand Lodge; 2. To protection while in the lawful exercise of its inherent rights; and 3. To the enjoyment of all powers conferred by the Grand Lodge upon any constituent Lodge.

FORFEITURE OF CHARTER.

The acts for which a charter may be forfeited and the Lodge dissolved are: 1. Contumacy to the authority of the Grand Master or Grand Lodge; 2. Departure from the original plan of Masonry, and a violation of the ancient landmarks; 3. Disobedience of the constitutions; 4. Ceasing to meet for one year or more; 5. Admitting clandestine Masons, or initiating known immoral candidates.

SURRENDERING THE CHARTER.

A Lodge may be dissolved by the voluntary surrender of its charter by its members, after special summons for that purpose, unless the minority opposed to such surrender consist of seven or more members, that number being the constitutional complement to *receive*, hence that number may *retain* the charter. This rule is now of almost universal practice in the United States.

SUSPENDING THE CHARTER.

The Grand Master may, for cause, arrest the charter of a Lodge, not to extend beyond the next annual communication of the Grand Lodge. Such suspension for the time arrests the work of the Lodge and prevents its meetings, but does not affect the Masonic standing of its members nor destroy the legality of its charter.

DUTIES OF A LODGE.

A Lodge by its acceptance of a charter, and its officers and members by their several Masonic obligations, are sacredly bound to obey the laws of Masonry. The duties of a Lodge, therefore, are: 1. To observe and preserve the ancient usages of Masonry; 2. To obey the constitution and regulations of the Grand Lodge.; 3. To render the Grand Master or his deputy all due respect and obedience; 4. Respectfully to hear all official communications from the Grand Lodge, the Grand Master, or any officer acting by their authority; 5. To be properly represented at the annual communications of the Grand Lodge; 6. To possess the proper jewels, clothing, etc., and a suitable seal; 7. To provide for its meetings a safe and suitable Lodge room; 8. To make, through its Secretary, the annual reports of its work and condition to Grand Lodge, and punctually to pay its annual dues.

For a persistent or inexcusable neglect by a Lodge, or of its officers, of any of the duties imposed; and for any deliberate violation of its obligations to Masonry or to the authority of the Grand Lodge or the edicts of the Grand Master, the charter thereof may be suspended or revoked.

AUTHORITY OVER SUSPENDED MASONS.

A Master Mason having been suspended for unmasonic conduct, and while under such suspension, may, upon new charges for repetition of the first offence, or for any other offence, be tried and expelled, or an additional term of suspension be inflicted if the offence so warrants, by the Lodge having personal jurisdiction over him.

GOVERNMENT OF THE LODGE.

There is no plainer or more definite law in Masonry than that the Master must preside over his Lodge; but in case of his absence, from any cause, the Senior Warden, and in the absence of both, the Junior Warden shall summon the Lodge to order, and succeed to all the powers and privileges of the Master; as though the Master himself were present, provided the warrant shall be present. In the absence of the Master or either of the Wardens the Lodge cannot be opened. A Past Master can only preside when the Master or one of the Wardens is present and opens the Lodge, after which he may call such Past Master to the chair. Whoever occupies the chair legally controls the Lodge. Even the Grand Master, if present, can exercise no authority until he has taken the chair and assumed the gavel.

OFFICERS OF A LODGE.

The prosperity, the success, and the usefulness of a Lodge, and its ability to discharge the duties and objects of Freemasonry, depend greatly upon the character and judgment of its officers.

The discipline of a Masonic Lodge, the order observed at its meetings, the obedience there exacted, and cheerfully rendered on the part of the brethren, make its government as nearly perfect as it is possible for any human institution to be. Intelligent and capable officers make good Lodges. It is the imperative duty of the officers of a Lodge to be careful, prudent, and conciliating, positive in requiring obedience to the law ; smoothing down all asperities of manner, spreading the cement of brotherly love and affection ; rendering to every one that due attention which should ever distinguish a band of brothers, and whilst by their own example they exhibit the beauties of the craft, they admonish with kindness, and reprehend with justice. Unity is the mainspring of Freemasonry. Destroy that, and the machinery will fall in pieces. It will be a difficult matter to preserve the links in the chain of unity unbroken, unless the Master pursues an accommodating policy, which may cause the brethren to be mutually pleased with each other's society, accompanied by an inflexible regard to discipline, which, while it allows freedom of action, will preserve inviolable the respectful submission that is due the Chair, as its undoubted and inalienable prerogative.

THE MASONIC JURIST.

The duties, responsibilities and prerogatives of the officers of a Lodge are now well defined (see Part I.), and consist of—1. A Master, who is styled Worshipful ; 2. A Senior Warden ; 3. A Junior Warden ; 4. A Treasurer ; 5. A Secretary ; 6. A Senior Deacon ; 7. A Junior Deacon ; 8. Two Stewards, or two Masters of Ceremonies (sometimes both); 9. A Tyler. In addition to the above, many Lodges are provided with a Chaplain, Marshal, Organist, and Board of Trustees.

PAST MASTERS.

By the term Past Masters, it must be understood to allude to those who have been legally elected Masters of chartered Lodges, served their term of office, and are recognized as *Actual* Past Masters, and who are distinguished from those who have been seated in the *chair* in a Royal Arch Chapter. Their privileges are such as may be expressly given by the Constitution of the Grand Lodge, and, in addition, they are qualified to install any Master elect, when requested to do so, and to be present at the qualification of a Master elected to the chair.

A Past Master is always eligible to re-election, without further service, to any office in the Lodge of which he is a member.

He is eligible as a proxy or representative of the Grand Master to perform any duty when that officer cannot attend.

As a courtesy, a Past Master is entitled to a seat in the east on the right of the acting Master.

A Chapter or *virtual* Past Master has no rights in a subordinate Lodge, and consequently cannot install a newly elected Master, or be present at the conferring of the Past Master's degree. This rule, however, is local, limited to a portion of the State jurisdictions.

Every Master Mason in good standing is the peer of a Past Master in matters of discipline, etc.

WORSHIPFUL MASTER'S ASSISTANT.

ELECTION AND INSTALLATION OF OFFICERS.

The election and appointment of officers shall be held annually, at such time as is prescribed by the Constitution of the Grand Lodge, or the by-laws of the Lodge (usually the regular meeting next preceding the festival of St. John the Evangelist, Dec. 27), and their installation must take place on the same evening, or within a reasonable period thereafter. Until such election and installation the incumbents in office shall hold over. No officer can be installed by proxy.

Previous to the annual election (if not already provided for in the by-laws), the Master should instruct the Secretary to call together the Lodge, notify every member of the amount of his indebtedness to the Lodge, and that in default of payment he will not be entitled to vote at such election.

Some opposition has been expressed against this doctrine on the constitutional provision that every member in good standing is entitled to one vote, but it is respectfully submitted that a member who fails to comply with the conditions of good standing, is not entitled to the immunities.

A Lodge having failed to elect its officers at the constitutional time, the Grand Master may grant a dispensation to hold an election at another time to complete the work of the Lodge.

At the election two tellers are appointed, who shall receive and count the ballots, and announce the result, under the supervision of the Master. A ballot represents a brother's vote, which is the expression of whatever opinion he may entertain.

Nominations of candidates for office are in order, and the candidate must receive a majority of all the votes cast to be legally declared elected.

When the constitution or the by-laws do not otherwise provide, the election of an officer may be taken by show of hands, or by a brother, selected for the purpose, casting one ballot, if there be no opposing candidate.

Every member of a Lodge in good standing is eligible to any office in his Lodge, except that of Master.

The members of a Lodge cannot prevent the installation of the Master elect by objecting to it, but the acting Master, in his judgment, may postpone the installation until the case can be submitted to the Grand Master.

FORMS OF MASONIC DOCUMENTS.

PETITION FOR A DISPENSATION FOR A NEW LODGE.

To the M. W. Grand Master of Masons of the State of ——:

The undersigned petitioners, being Ancient Free and Accepted Master Masons, having the prosperity of the Fraternity at heart, and willing to exert their best endeavors to promote and diffuse the genuine principles of Masonry, respectfully represent—That they are desirous of forming a new Lodge in the —— of ——, county of ——, and State of ——, to be named ——, No. —. They therefore pray for letters of Dispensation, to empower them to assemble as a regular Lodge, to discharge the duties of Masonry in a regular and constitutional manner, according to the original forms of the Order, and the regulations of the Grand Lodge. They have nominated and do recommend Brother A B to be the first Master; Brother C D to be the first Senior Warden, and Brother E F to be the first Junior Warden, of said Lodge. If the prayer of this petition shall be granted, they promise a strict conformity to the edicts of the Grand Master, and the constitution, laws, and regulations of the Grand Lodge.

(This petition must be signed by not less than seven Master Masons, recommended by one or two Lodges. The constitutional fee must be forwarded to the Grand Master or Grand Secretary. On receipt of the Dispensation, the Master, Wardens, and brethren named therein will assemble, and open a Master's Lodge in due form. The three officers named must be present. But a Lodge is not constituted, or officers installed, until a charter is granted.)

WORSHIPFUL MASTER'S ASSISTANT.

RECOMMENDATION FOR NEW LODGE.

To the M. W. Grand Master of Masons of ———:

At a regular meeting of ——— Lodge, No. —, holden at ———, on the ——— day of ———, 19—, the petition of several Master Masons, praying for a Dispensation to open a new Lodge at ———, in the county of ———, State of ———, was duly laid before the Lodge, when it was

Resolved, That this Lodge, being fully satisfied that the petitioners are Master Masons in good standing, and being willing to vouch for their Masonic abilities, does therefore recommend that the Dispensation prayed for be granted to them.

A true copy of the records.

——— ———, *Secretary*.

(Seal.)

FORM OF DISPENSATION FOR NEW LODGE.

Grand Lodge of Free and Accepted Masons of the State of ———.

To all to whom these presents may come, GREETING:

WHEREAS, a petition has been presented to me by Brothers ———, residing within this jurisdiction, praying, on account of the convenience of their respective dwellings, and for other good reasons, for a Dispensation to empower them to assemble as a legal Lodge, to discharge the duties of Masonry in the several degrees of Entered Apprentice, Fellow Craft, and Master Mason, in a regular and constitutional manner, according to the ancient forms of the Fraternity, and the constitution and regulations of this Grand Lodge;

And, WHEREAS, The said petitioners have been recommended to me as Master Masons in good standing by the Worshipful Master, Wardens and brethren of ——— Lodge, No. —, under our jurisdiction; Therefore, I, ——— ———, Grand Master of the Grand Lodge of Free and Accepted Masons of the State of ———, by virtue of the authority in me vested, do hereby grant this my Dispensation, authorizing and empowering our trusty and well-beloved brethren aforesaid, to form and open a new Lodge in the ——— of ———, in county of ———, and State of ———, to be called ——— Lodge, and therein to admit and make Entered Apprentices, Fellow Crafts, and Master Masons, in accordance with the ancient usages and customs of the Fraternity, obeying in all things the constitution, laws, and edicts of this Grand Lodge, and not otherwise.

And I do hereby appoint our worthy brother, A B, to be the first Master; Brother C D to be the first Senior Warden, and Brother E F to be the first Junior Warden of said new Lodge.

And it shall be their duty, and they are hereby required to return this Dispensation with a correct transcript of all proceedings had under the authority of the same, together with an attested copy of their by-laws, to our Grand Lodge, at its next annual communication, for examination, and such further action as shall then be deemed wise and proper.

This Dispensation to continue in full force till the annual communication aforesaid, unless sooner revoked by me.

(Seal.) In testimony whereof, I have hereunto set my hand and seal, this —— day of ——, A.D. 19—.

—————— ——————, *Grand Master.*

COMMISSION TO CONSTITUTE A LODGE AND INSTALL ITS OFFICERS.

BY THE M. W. GRAND MASTER OF MASONS OF THE STATE OF ——.

To all to whom these presents may come, GREETING:

WHEREAS, the Most Worshipful Grand Lodge of ——, at its late annual communication, empowered, by warrant of constitution regularly issued, A B, Master, C D, Senior Warden, and E F, Junior Warden, and their successors, to assemble as a regular Lodge, at ——; and ancient Masonic usage requires that said Lodge shall be duly constituted;

Now, therefore, know ye, that I, —— ——, Grand Master of Masons of the State of ——, reposing special trust and confidence in the skill, prudence and ability of Brother ——, Past Master (or W. Master) of —— Lodge, No. —, being unable to attend in person, have authorized and empowered our said Worshipful Brother to constitute, in form, the new Lodge at ——, to be known and designated as —— Lodge, No. —, and to install the officers of said new Lodge according to the ancient usages of the craft; and for so doing this shall be his sufficient warrant.

Given under our hand and seal, at the City of ——, on the — day of ——, A.L. 59—, A. D. 19—.

—— ——, *Grand Master.* (Seal.)

This form may be readily adapted to the appointing of a proxy for any other purpose.

COMMISSION FOR REPRESENTATIVE (OTHER THAN MASTER AND WARDEN).

To all whom these presents may concern, Greeting:

Know ye, that we, the members of —— Lodge, No. —, reposing trust and confidence in the fidelity, skill, and Masonic abilities of our Worthy Brother ——, do hereby constitute and appoint him our representative in the Grand Lodge of ——, in case of the absence of the Worshipful Master and Wardens, at its next annual communication, to be held at —— on the — day of ——, 19—, empowering him to act in our behalf, hereby ratifying and confirming whatsoever he may do in said capacity.

(Seal.) In testimony whereof, the Master of our said Lodge has set his hand, and caused the Secretary to affix the seal of the Lodge thereto, this — day of ——, A.L. 59—, A.D. 19—.

Attest: —— ——, *Master.*
—— ——, *Secretary.*

COMMISSION FOR PROXY OF A MASTER, OR EITHER OF THE WARDENS OF A LODGE.

To whom these presents may concern, Greeting:

Know ye, that I, —— ——, Master of —— Lodge, No. —, held at —— in the county of ——, do hereby constitute and appoint our worthy Brother —— my proxy in the Grand Lodge of ——, empowering him to act in my behalf, and hereby confirming and ratifying whatsoever he may do in said capacity.

(Seal.) Given under my hand and the seal of said Lodge, this — day of ——, A.L. 59—, A.D. 19—.

Attest: —— ——, *Master.*
—— ——. *Secretary.*

FORMS OF MASONIC DOCUMENTS.

PETITION FOR INITIATION AND MEMBERSHIP.

To the W. Master, Wardens and Members of —— *Lodge, No.* —, *F. and A. Masons:*

The petition of the undersigned respectfully represents, that entertaining a favorable opinion of your ancient and honorable institution, being unbiased by the improper solicitation of friends, and uninfluenced by mercenary or other improper motives, he is desirous of being admitted and becoming a member of your Lodge, if found worthy, promising a cheerful conformity to the usages and customs of the Order.

Place of residence is ——; age is — years; and his occupation is ——. (Signed), —— ——.
Recommended by —— ——,
—— ——.

APPLICATION FOR AFFILIATION.

To the W. Master, Wardens and Members of —— *Lodge, No.* —:

The undersigned, a Master Mason in good standing, and last a member of —— Lodge, No. —, located at ——, State of ——, ——, respectfully prays to be admitted to membership in your Lodge.

Dated, ——, 19—.
Signed, —— ——.
Recommended by —— ——.

REPORT OF COMMITTEE ON APPLICATION.

The Committee upon the application of ——, report favorably (or unfavorably).

Signed, —— ——,
—— ——, } *Committee.*
Dated, ——, 19—. —— ——.

NOTICE FOR PAYMENT OF DUES.

Hall of —— Lodge, No. —. ——, 19.
Brother —— :

Take notice, that your Lodge dues for the present year are now due, and payable on or before the ——.

WORSHIPFUL MASTER'S ASSISTANT.

The amount is $—, on payment of which I shall be pleased to hand you a receipt. Fraternally,
(Seal.) ———— ————, *Secretary*.

TO SHOW CAUSE WHY MEMBER SHOULD NOT PAY DUES, OR BE STRUCK FROM ROLL OF MEMBERS.

HALL OF —— LODGE, No. —.
——, 19—.

To Brother ———:

You will take notice that you are required to pay the sum of $—, being the amount of dues owing by you to —— Lodge, No. —, or show cause at the next stated communication of the Lodge, to be held on the — day of ——, 19—, at — o'clock, P.M., why your name should not be stricken from the roll of members, as provided by sec. — of the by-laws of this Lodge.

By order of the Lodge.

Seal.) ———— ————, *Secretary*.

APPLICATION FOR DEGREES BY A PERSON WHO HAS BEEN ELECTED BY ANOTHER LODGE, OR HAS RECEIVED ONE OR MORE DEGREES THEREIN.

To the W. Master, Wardens and Members of —— *Lodge, No.* —, *F. and A. M.:*

The undersigned respectfully shows that, on or about the — day of ——, 19—, he was duly elected as a candidate for the three degrees of Masonry by —— Lodge, No. —, located at ——, where he then resided, and thereafter duly received the first degree (or first and second degrees) of Masonry in said Lodge; that, for the sake of greater convenience (or other good cause), your petitioner prays that he may receive the remaining degrees in your Lodge.

The consent of —— Lodge is hereto annexed (or show it to be impossible to obtain consent).

Dated, ——, 19—.

Signed, ———— ————.

Recommender, ———— ————.

FORMS OF MASONIC DOCUMENTS.

APPLICATION FOR DISPENSATION TO AVOID DELAY.

HALL OF —— LODGE, No. —.
——, 19—.

To the M. W. —— *Grand Master of Masons of the State of* ——:

M. W. SIR: Mr. A B, having duly presented his application to be initiated, passed, and raised to the sublime degree of Master Mason in —— Lodge, No. —, and imperative circumstances [state the nature thereof], making it necessary that he should proceed without delay, respectfully asks that a dispensation be granted, empowering said Lodge to confer said degrees as soon as may be practicable.

Signed,   A—— B——.

I, the Master of —— Lodge, No. —, certify that the application of A B presents a case of emergency, and recommend that the dispensation asked for be granted, and that he may receive the degrees accordingly, if found worthy.

(Seal.)   Signed,   ———— ————, *Master.*
            ———— ————, *Secretary.*

DISPENSATION TO AVOID DELAY.

OFFICE OF THE GRAND MASTER OF MASONS.
——, 19—.

To whom these presents shall come, GREETING:

Application having been made to permit —— Lodge, No. —, under this jurisdiction, to initiate, pass and raise A B to the sublime degree of Master Mason, who is unable, for certain reasons, to wait the time prescribed by our regulations, and the said Lodge consenting thereto;

Now, know ye, that I, ———— ————, Grand Master of Masons in and for said State, by virtue of the power and authority in me vested, do hereby authorize and empower said Lodge to proceed and confer the degrees without delay on said A B, in accordance with the ancient usages and customs of Freemasonry, and not otherwise; and for so doing these presents shall be their sufficient warrant.

(Seal.)   Given under my hand, and the private seal of Grand Master, this — day of ——, 19—.

———— ————, *Grand Master.*

WORSHIPFUL MASTER'S ASSISTANT.

NOTICE OF APPOINTMENT OF COMMITTEE.

HALL OF —— LODGE, No. —. ——, 19—.

Brother —— —— :

Take notice, that at a stated communication of this Lodge, held this date, you were appointed on a committee to examine into and report upon ——. The committee appointed consists of Bros. ——.

Report to be called for at next stated communication.

Fraternally,

—— ——, *Secretary*.

DISPENSATION AUTHORIZING LODGE TO CONTINUE ITS LABORS AFTER LOSS OF ITS CHARTER.

To all to whom these presents shall come, GREETING:

Know ye, that whereas it hath been represented to us by W. Brother ——, Master of —— Lodge, No. —, of said Lodge, that the charter of said Lodge has been lost (by fire or otherwise), and that the same cannot be found; and, whereas, the Master, Wardens and members are desirous of continuing the labors of said Lodge;

Now, therefore, by virtue of the power and authority in us vested, as Grand Master of Masons in the State of ——, we do hereby authorize and empower the said Master, Wardens and members of —— Lodge, No. —, to continue their Masonic labors, and to perform all the functions of a regular Lodge in as full and complete a manner as if their charter was still in existence, until the next annual communication of the M. W. Grand Lodge, to which this dispensation shall be returned.

(Seal.) Witness our hand and seal, at the city of ——, the — day of ——, A.L. 59—, A.D. 19—.

—— ——, *Grand Master*.

DISPENSATION TO ELECT A MASTER.

THE MOST WORSHIPFUL GRAND LODGE OF —— FREE AND ACCEPTED MASONS.

To whom these presents may come, GREETING:

Whereas, I have received official information that the office of

FORMS OF MASONIC DOCUMENTS.

Master of —— Lodge, No. —, has become vacant by the (death or permanent removal from the jurisdiction) of —— ——, late Master thereof, and it is represented to me that it is important to the welfare of said Lodge that said office shall be filled, and a Master of said Lodge duly elected to supply said vacancy: Now, Know Ye, that I, —— ——, Grand Master of Masons of the State of ——, do issue this, my special dispensation, authorizing and empowering said Lodge to proceed to fill said vacancy by the election of a brother to serve as Master until his successor is duly elected.

Given under my hand and private seal, at ——, this — day of ——, A.L. 59—, A.D. 19—.

—— ——, *Grand Master.* (Seal.)

A dispensation for the above purpose is seldom called for. The almost universal rule prevails, that in the absence of the Master, the Senior Warden assumes the responsibilities and duties of the Master.

COMMISSION TO DEDICATE A MASONIC HALL.

THE MOST WORSHIPFUL GRAND LODGE OF —— FREE AND ACCEPTED MASONS.

To all to whom these presents shall come, GREETING:

Whereas, —— Lodge, No. —, in the —— of ——, has prepared and furnished a room, in which the members thereof desire to hold their meetings in future; and it is meet and proper that the same should be dedicated to Masonic uses with appropriate ceremonies: Now, Know Ye, that I, —— ——, Grand Master of Masons of the State of ——, reposing special trust and confidence in the Masonic skill and ability of our Worshipful Brother ——, Master (or Past Master) of —— Lodge, No. —, have thought proper (being unable to attend in person), to nominate and appoint him to perform the ceremonies of dedication, according to the ancient usages of the craft, and for so doing this shall be his sufficient warrant. And he is hereby required to report his acts and doings in the above service to this office.

Given under my hand and the private seal of the Grand Master, at ——, this — day of ——, A.L. 59—, A.D. 19—.

—— ——, *Grand Master.* (Seal.)

WORSHIPFUL MASTER'S ASSISTANT.

COMMISSION TO LAY A CORNER-STONE.

To whom these presents shall come, GREETING:

Whereas, —— Lodge, No. —, in the —— of ——, has undertaken to erect a building in which the members thereof propose to hold their future meetings, and having requested that the corner-stone be laid with the appropriate ceremonies of the Order:

Now, Know Ye, that I, —— ——, Grand Master of Masons in the State of ——, reposing especial trust and confidence in the Masonic skill and ability of our Worshipful Brother ——, a Past Master of —— Lodge, No. — (R. W. Brother if a Grand Officer), have thought proper, being unable to attend in person, to nominate and appoint him to lay the corner-stone of the proposed building according to the ancient usages of the craft, and for so doing this shall be his sufficient warrant. And he will report his acts and doings hereunto to this office.

Given under my hand and the private seal of Grand Master, at ——, this —— day of ——, A.D. 19—, A.L. 59—.

—— ——, *Grand Master.* (Seal.)

PETITION FOR CHANGING LOCATION OF LODGE.

HALL OF —— LODGE, No. —.   ——, 19—.

To the M. W. Grand Master of the Grand Lodge of ——:

At the last regular meeting of this Lodge, the desire was expressed, and the sense of the Lodge taken in favor of removal from the present place of meeting to ——. Your permission for such removal is therefore respectfully solicited, and the same having been obtained, the further conditions in section — of the by-laws shall be carefully complied with.

(Seal.)   —— ——, *Master.*

Attest: —— ——, *Secretary.*

APPOINTMENT OF DISTRICT DEPUTY GRAND MASTER.

THE GRAND LODGE OF —— FREE AND ACCEPTED MASONS.

To all whom it may concern, GREETING:

Know Ye, That reposing special trust and confidence in the

FORMS OF MASONIC DOCUMENTS.

Masonic skill and ability of our Worthy Brother ——, a Past Master of —— Lodge, No. —, I do hereby appoint him to the office of District Deputy Grand Master of the —— District of this Grand Jurisdiction, composed of the counties of ——, and embracing the several subordinate Lodges therein. He will be obeyed and respected accordingly.

This Commission is to continue in force (unless sooner revoked) until the next annual communication of the Grand Lodge.

Given under my hand and the private seal of the Grand Master, this — day of ——, A.L. 59—, A.D. 19—.

—— ——, *Grand Master.* (Seal.)

APPLICATION FOR A DIMIT.

To the W. Master, Wardens and Brethren of —— Lodge, No. —, Free and Accepted Masons:

The undersigned, now a member of the Lodge, and having paid all known dues and assessments, requests that he may be dimitted from the Lodge. Signed,

Dated, ——, 19—.   —— ——

DIMIT.

FREE AND ACCEPTED MASONS.

—— LODGE, No. —.

Acknowledging the jurisdiction of the Grand Lodge of the State of ——, to all whom it may concern, GREETING: This certifies that Bro. ——, whose name appears in the margin of this dimit, is a Master Mason, and was a member of this Lodge, in good standing, and having paid all dues, and otherwise complied with all legal requirements of the Lodge, we do cordially commend him to the fraternal regard of all true Free and Accepted Masons, wherever dispersed around the globe.

In testimony whereof, we have caused this dimit to be signed by the Master, and the seal of the Lodge to be attached, this — day of ——, A.D. 19—, A.L. 59—.   —— ——, *Master.*

—— ——, *Secretary.*

Ne Varietur ....

(Seal.)

217